FROM PRINT
TO STITCH

TIPS AND TECHNIQUES FOR HAND-PRINTING AND STITCHING ON FABRIC

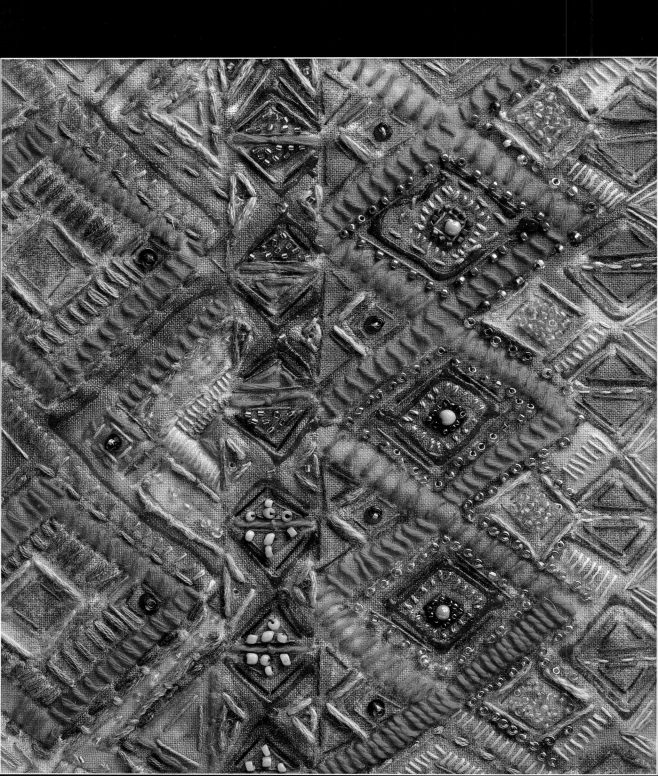

FROM PRINT
TO STITCH

TIPS AND TECHNIQUES FOR HAND-PRINTING AND STITCHING ON FABRIC

JANET EDMONDS

SEARCH PRESS

First published in Great Britain 2010

Search Press Limited
Wellwood, North Farm Road,
Tunbridge Wells, Kent TN2 3DR

Text copyright © Janet Edmonds 2010

Photographs by Roddy Paine Photographic Studio
Photographs and design copyright
© Search Press Ltd 2010

ISBN: 978-1-84448-459-1

Acknowledgements
I would like to thank everyone at Search Press,
especially Katie Sparkes and
Roz Dace, and photographers Roddy Paine
and Gavin Sawyer, for helping me to create
this book. Thanks are also due to my family,
who have supported my endeavours, and to
my students everywhere, who have shown
such enthusiasm and encouragement.

Publisher's note
All the step-by-step photographs in this book
feature the author, Janet Edmonds, demonstrating
mixed media craftwork. No models have been used.

Printed in Malaysia

Page 1
*A wooden block print is embellished with couching using a thick raw
silk thread and a finer cotton thread to hold it down. The centre of
the shape is filled with whipped and woven straight stitches.*

Pages 2 and 3
*Straight stitches and couching are used to embellish this print made
from triangles and oblongs. Threads are hand-dyed silk and cottons
with beads to highlight the centres.*

Page 5
*A soft-cut lino block was developed from the theme 'Objects on a
shelf' (see pages 24–26). Part of a plate with a patterned edge and
a hanging cup form the design, which is decorated using straight
stitches and chain stitch with couched lines at either side.*

CONTENTS

Introduction

A print may be described as the mark that is made when one wet and sticky surface is transferred to another surface. An obvious statement perhaps, but here is a process that has generated some very beautiful and complex images from the earliest times. There are many examples of prints left behind throughout history that are clues to understanding the world as it has evolved over many millennia. Imprints of the feet of animals and humans in wet mud, hand prints left on the walls of caves made using earth pigments, or decoration of the surface of pottery by imprinting texture from fabric is all evidence that the idea of print has been around for a very long time.

A print from a collagraph block made with bubblewrap is enhanced with free machine embroidery using a metallic thread. The background fabric was coloured with printing ink left over after a print session.

This sponge print was machine stitched with a narrow zigzag worked freely. The spaces are then cut away and the fabric applied to a textured print.

The development of paper in China in 100 B.C. meant that prints could be taken from stone inscriptions. The following stage, in 600 A.D., saw wood blocks developed for books that contained complex imagery, including text. When the printing press was invented in Germany by Johannes Gutenburg in the fifteenth century, the printed word became more available and ordinary men and women were able to access information and learnt to read and write. Once man realised that he could transfer signs and symbols to paper and repeat them over and over again to create books, it was the start of the sharing and dissemination of knowledge as we know it today.

The earliest examples of print on cloth date from 1000 to 800 B.C. in Egypt and 220 B.C. in China, where incised wood blocks were used to make printed patterns. Olmec Indians, an ancient Indian people of

These three stitched prints have been developed from a drawing of patterned cloth (see page 27). They have been printed using the same block but in different colours, and stitched with a mixture of hand and machine stitching. This demonstrates how it is possible to achieve a completely different effect using the same print block.

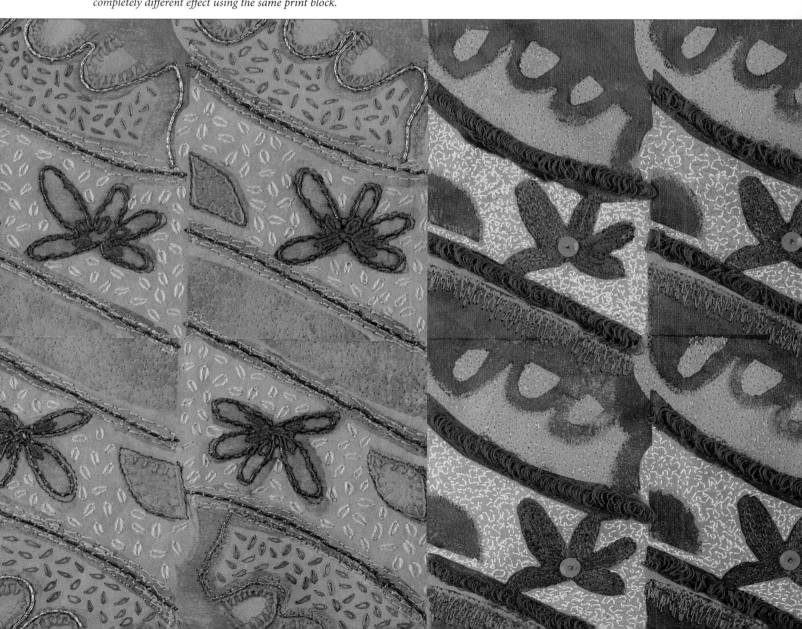

Mexico, living from 1200 to 100 B.C., baked clay tubes with relief patterns and used them to print repeat patterns on their skin and on bark surfaces.

Prints can be made using very simple equipment and materials, without the need for a press, but printing can also be a very technical and highly refined process too. In this book, I aim to show that simple printing can be very accessible and can lead on to the development of more complexity by combining methods and processes.

There are many excellent books available on creating prints, and also books devoted to stitch. In this book, I intend to explore print in combination with stitch, to show how to decorate fabric, and how the printed surface may be further embellished with stitch to enrich and complement the prints, without losing the print completely.

The materials and equipment that I use are all readily available and the processes are uncomplicated. I like to recycle paper and card where possible and to reuse fabric where appropriate. Simple everyday items can often be utilised with print in mind. I have used the end of a pencil, an old fork, cotton reels, rubber washers and packing materials to make prints. With concern for the environment and the need to protect our own health and safety, it is important to be aware of what is in the paint, ink and cleaning fluids that are used in this process. I prefer to use the common substances that we are all familiar with rather than chemically hazardous ones that are difficult to dispose of and that might be harmful to work with. A purpose-designed studio will take account of these issues but when working in the domestic environment, consideration should be given to what materials are used and how equipment is stored so that others in that environment are not put at risk.

Materials and tools

Textile artists will most likely already have a ready supply of basic equipment, fabric and paper, but there are a few other requirements that may need to be gathered together. One essential requirement is a suitable place to work. In an ideal world we would all have studio space to explore our creative activities, but not everyone has that perfect solution. I worked for many years on my dining-room table before I made space in my garage, and I had to develop a clean and tidy method of working, keeping mess to a minimum and making sure that everything was properly cleaned up after a working session. A sturdy table covered with a protective material that can be washed down and space to lay out or hang up drying prints are the main criteria.

HEALTH AND SAFETY

Usual common sense should prevail when working with art and craft materials. In particular, care should be taken when using cutting equipment, metallic powders, inks and paints. Follow manufacturer's instructions when applicable and protect surfaces from spilt paint and scratches from equipment. Above all, protect yourself by wearing an overall and protective gloves, and a mask if fine dust is involved. Be aware of anything that may cause allergy or discomfort.

If you work in an orderly manner, accidents and spills can be kept to a minium or avoided altogether.

A selection showing the range of papers and card that I use for printing paper and fabrics.

Papers

In order to achieve a good print on paper or fabric, it is necessary for
the surface to be completely smooth and flat. Cartridge paper, available
either as loose sheets or in a sketchbook, is needed for trying out prints
and for recording and developing ideas. Artists who want to concentrate
on achieving good prints would want to print on to good-quality paper
designed specially for print, such as Somerset paper, which is available
through print makers' suppliers. Tracing paper is used for tracing off images
developed for motifs, and is a useful method of reversing an image such as
one that includes text as it can simply be turned over. Almost any other
kind of paper, such as photocopy paper, brown paper, wrapping paper,
tissue, old envelopes, advertising leaflets and fliers, can be brought into use
when making blocks for collagraphs (see page 84). Photocopies are useful
for cutting images from to use as templates.

Card

I collect card from a variety of sources such as off-cuts from mount card or
grey board, the back of old sketchbooks or cardboard cartons. Foam core
board gives thickness when needed. All these are useful depending on the
purpose for which you intend to use them.

Inks and paints

Printing ink

There are many brands of ink out there in the marketplace, but the make is immaterial so long as it fits the criteria needed for printing on to fabric, that is, that it is thick and sticky and designed to be used on fabric. It is worth mentioning the difference between ink and printing ink. Ink used for drawing or adding washes is thin, watery, flows easily, and dries relatively quickly, whereas ink for printing is thicker and has a sticky feel to it. It often takes a while to dry, at which stage it should be ironed to fix it to the fabric. Follow the manufacturer's instructions for temperature and duration of heat.

Acrylic paint

I often use acrylic paint for printing on to paper, adding fabric medium to slow the drying time when needed, although this is not often as I have usually worked out in advance what I am going to print.

Fabric paint

This is paint specially designed to be used on fabric; it does not make the fabric stiff, as is the case with acrylic paints which alter the handling characteristics of the fabric. It is usually the consistency of thick cream and sits on the surface of fabric rather than soaking right through, although if the fabric is fine and enough pressure is applied when printing, the paint will be forced into the fibres and be seen on the reverse side. By experimenting, you will find a brand that you like. As always, follow the manufacturer's instructions for heat setting the paint.

Tools and materials for fabric painting.

Fabric medium

Also known as block printing medium. A medium can be added to fabric paint or acrylic to thicken it or to extend the working time. It also controls the bleeding of colour that has been thinned with water and can improve the softness of the fabric after printing. The addition of a medium to a fabric paint will make it more transparent, which is useful when over-printing. Some mediums are available to mix with metallic powders. Again, there are many types on the market and preference will come with experimentation.

Fabrics

Printing on to fabric requires it to be flat and without slub or nap. Any cotton, linen or silk should give a good result provided it fits this description. I find it works best when freshly washed and ironed. I seldom, if ever, use man-made fabrics for print but it is worth experimenting, while remembering that man-made fabrics come into their own when used for transfer printing, though this is not covered in this book. However, some of the newer fabrics such as Suede FX, which has a very flat but soft surface, gives very good prints with excellent definition.

Fabric can be coloured or not, as preferred. I use both depending on the effect that I want to achieve. I use Procion dyes to colour my fabric. These can be easily sourced from your local hardware shop or from specialist suppliers. If I want to adjust the colour or add some contrast colour, I will use fabric paint or silk paint.

A selection of dyed fabrics.

Tools

Most of the equipment that I use is quite basic and can be obtained easily through mail order, art shops or your local DIY store, but there are a few essential items that may not be so obvious.

Cutting equipment

You will need a good-quality craft knife or scalpel for cutting card and plastic erasers. Use it with a metal ruler and a self-healing cutting mat. It is a good idea to have some spare blades as they do blunt quite quickly when doing a lot of cutting into heavy card.

A self-healing cutting mat and scalpel.

Rollers or brayers

It is not essential to have a roller for printing but it would be impossible to spread out the ink on the plate for monoprinting without one (see page 68), or to ink up a large block. It is therefore a very useful tool and I would not be without one. Apart from rolling out ink and mixing paint colours, it can be used to exert even pressure on the back of a block when applying it on to fabric, in addition to adding the ink to the block. Good ones are expensive but cheaper ones are available that have interchangeable rollers and handles. This can save much cleaning up time and would be a good choice for beginners or for those who do not print very often. It is always possible to upgrade when your confidence and expertise increases. Care should be taken not to leave paint or printing ink to dry on the roller as it will result in an uneven surface on the rubber.

It is possible to obtain textured rollers from DIY stores. These are designed to add texture to wall surfaces but they make an excellent addition to your equipment list, providing the means to add texture to your fabric before printing shape or pattern. It is also possible to make your own, too, by wrapping string or strips of torn fabric around a card roll and fixing the ends with a dab of glue.

A selection of rollers.

Print surfaces

It is important to have a smooth, firm surface for printing and, when printing on to fabric, a surface with a bit of 'give' will allow the block to be pressed into it and so give a clearer image. A slightly padded surface can be set up using a piece of blanket or wadding, a table protector or a sheet of foam. A foam mouse mat could be used, but ideally the surface should be able to be wiped clean after printing.

Printing surfaces.

Printing plate

Anything with a smooth, shiny, non-absorbent surface can be used for mixing inks or paint, rolling out the ink and then transferring the ink to the print block via the roller.

Printing plate, colour shapers and palette knife.

The printing plate is also used to roll out ink for monoprinting. A sheet of acetate or polypropylene will do the job, or even a Formica chopping board, provided that it has not been used for chopping. The most professional but expensive surface is toughened glass with the edges ground smooth. This is easily cleaned and doesn't scratch readily but is heavy if it has to be moved about. It can also be broken if dropped, causing risk of cuts and scratches and damage to surroundings.

Additional tools

A palette knife is useful to mix printing inks. Colour shapers have a tip made from silicone rubber and can be used to mix, blend and move paint around on the plate prior to printing. Paper scissors, pens, pencils and a variety of brushes are basic equipment for artists. Disposable plastic spoons are invaluable for spooning inks from jars and can be thrown away when they become discoloured or coated with paint.

Lino-cutting tools.

A set of lino-cutting tools with a variety of cutting nibs are essential for cutting lino blocks and will be further described later in the book (see page 62).

Scissors.

Blocks

These can be made from a wide choice of materials and it is now possible to buy specialist blocks designed for printing. I prefer to make mine by re-using offcuts of mount board or the thick card from the back of sketchbooks. Funky Foam sheets can be cut to shape and stuck to card or wood block. A design that requires a linear treatment can be made from parcel string stuck to a piece of wood or card. A variety of other ready-made objects found around the home can be brought into use as shapes to print from. Pencil erasers, for example, make excellent blocks and are very easy to cut.

Other items for block printing include PVA glue, used to stick a variety of surfaces together, and masking tape, which makes a very efficient resist when stuck to paper or fabric when printing with textures. Varnish and button polish seal the porous surfaces of blocks, making them more durable, and sponge pieces can be used for inking up small blocks.

Lino and vinyl

These materials are used to create blocks for printing. More information will be provided in the relevant chapter (see page 60).

A selection of materials for use as printing blocks, including foam, vinyl, sponge, balsa wood, card and a pencil eraser.

Sewing materials

You will need a general sewing kit (shown right), including pins and a variety of needles: sharps, embroidery and tapestry. A stiletto and a couronne stick are both useful accessories, as is a pair of small, sharp embroidery scissors. Many stitchers like to work with a thimble and have the work under tension in an embroidery frame. Both these items are optional and a matter of personal choice. I don't often use either but every now and again an instance arises when one or other or both are necessary so it is useful to have them. On occasions, a small pair of pliers can be handy for pulling the needle through tough or thick fabric. I find this saves stress on the fingers and obviates the need for excessive grip.

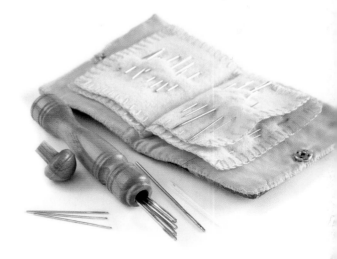

Your sewing machine should have both straight and swing-needle functions, and the ability to drop the feed dog or cover it so that free machine stitching can be accessed. A darning foot is a must-have attachment and a metal embroidery frame essential for some tasks. Other sewing feet that are nice to have but not essential are tailor's tacking feet and cording feet.

A collection of hand-embroidery threads may include cotton perle thread, soft cotton, crochet cotton, silk and linen threads, and lustrous rayon threads in a variety of thicknesses. A selection of these is shown right. Fine wool gives a matt effect and provides contrast. There is a wealth of choice in the marketplace, but aim to acquire a variety in terms of colour, tone, weight and surface quality, that is, matt, shiny, or having a sheen to it, rough, smooth and metallic. It is hard to resist buying thread when the colours and textures are so inviting and seductive. I have a mantra that says that if I don't intend to use it then don't buy it. In practice, I dye most of my fabrics and threads as and when I need them and I find this avoids excessive waste and reduces storage problems. I can also have a subtle range of one colour or a combination of several. There are many good books available that will show you how to colour fabric and thread so I don't intend to cover those skills in this book. Suffice to say that I use Procion dyes for cotton and linen, and acid dyes for silk, wool and rayon.

It takes time to build a collection of machine-embroidery threads, but aim to have light, medium and dark colours and a variety of types: cotton, silk, rayon or matt. Don't forget ordinary sewing thread as this can give a contrast to the lustre of the embroidery ones and it is usually cheaper.

Other sewing equipment will be explained as and when it crops up throughout the book.

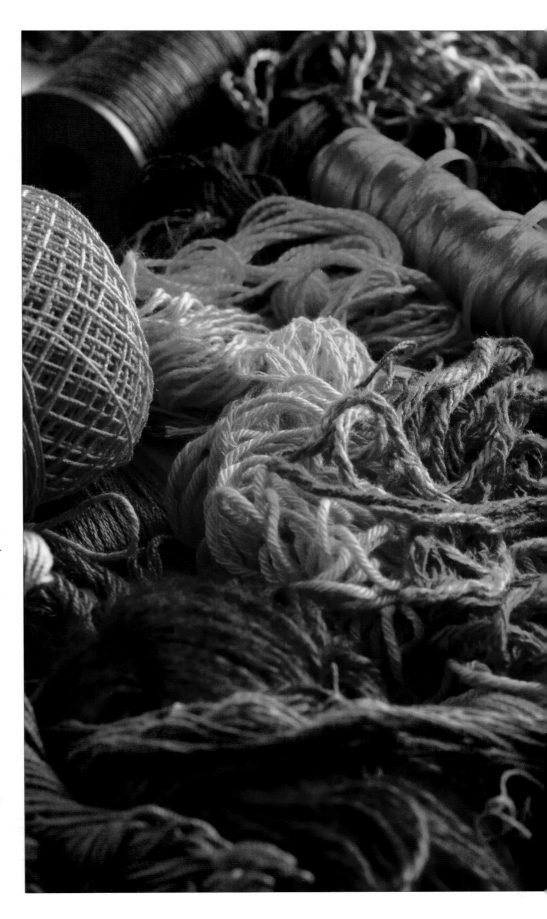

Developing a theme

The journey from the first idea through to a finished item can be a daunting one, especially for those who are new to it, but the creative process is hugely rewarding when simple steps are taken in a logical sequence. It is a process that all can learn, and a good way to start is to really look, and to practise how to record what you see. It is a good idea to record colour relationships, shape and pattern, texture, line and form, as these are the building blocks of design. Simple marks on paper can suggest stitching and, when repeated, can grow into something more complex.

I seldom go looking for ideas as they usually seem to find me and draw me in. At the beginning of the process, I am unaware of how or when I might use the information I am gathering. I just know that a drawing will lead me to additional exciting places. I can appreciate that beginners may find it difficult to understand that it is not necessary to know in advance the detailed nature of the process as they may be impatient to know what comes next, but some degree of spontaneity adds the freedom to play with ideas and allows them to lead you. With practice, you will come to recognise potential when you see it.

Ideas can come from the very ordinary and mundane things that surround us, such as a few bottles or jars set next to each other, a pair of scissors or the shape of a flower. These are common, everyday items, and half the battle is being able to see their potential. What is needed to make a satisfactory print is a subject, a shape and some idea of colour.

If you have a photograph or a picture of something that appeals to you in a book or magazine, you could trace a shape from it to turn into a print block. The magazine picture shown at the top of this page was the inspiration for a monoprint that was further developed using the rough shape of the flower as a resist. The paper resist was added to the print after being used.

Creating a motif

The basis of all pattern is the repeat of an element or motif. This may be for surface decoration on a flat plane, or the fabric of a physical structure or form. For pattern to be visually appealing and to be able to build into more complex patterns, an underlying network of guidelines exists which may be invisible or form part of the pattern itself. Pattern is made up of negative and positive areas and the two most important aspects of working with pattern are the motifs (positive) and the spaces in between (negative).

What you should be looking for

Simplicity: what you should be looking for is a simple shape. Detail can be left out at the initial print stage and added later using repetition and stitching to create a more complex image. You are not trying to replicate exactly what you are seeing but to take inspiration from it. I often observe among students that an image may be rejected too soon; they are judging it before really seeing the potential of it. My advice is to try several images and then choose the one you like.

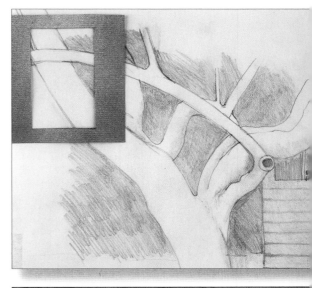

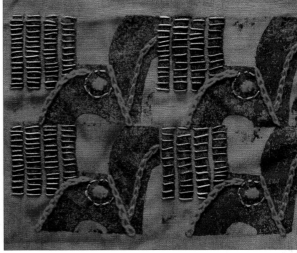

This motif began as a simple drawing of a tree beside a shed in my garden (top). I blocked in the background to accentuate the form of the tree and kept the outline of the tree itself to a simple line. I recorded very little texture or shadow. I made a viewfinder by cutting a hole in a piece of paper. This I placed over the drawing in order to select areas that would make a good motif. Some were more successful than others but all could be developed as blocks for print, and they also work well together (see left).

I selected one motif and made an eraser block from it, first making a drawing to decide which areas were to be cut away. I used the block to print a design on to fabric, which I then stitched by hand (above).

When the drawing was transferred to the eraser, the image became slightly foreshortened as the eraser was shorter than my drawing. To get around this problem, the viewfinder could be made to the same proportions as the eraser.

Contrast: when deciding on the motif, or shape, what you are looking for is some contrast in the mass. This is the space that the shape takes up on the page, so you will have some large areas and some smaller ones within the shape you have chosen. It also helps if you have a contrast between the positive shape (your chosen shape) and the negative space, which is the background.

Asymmetry: it is worth remembering, too, that asymmetrical motifs build more interesting patterns. Try to avoid lots of little shapes that are all the same size as the background shapes. If you think your motif is bland or uninteresting, this is probably why. The solution is to change it so that there is more contrast.

Complementary colours (blue and orange) are used for the printed fabric bag. The print is outlined with a straight machine stitch and the spaces filled with a machined texture. Machine cords (see page 122) are twisted together to make a strap. The bag is lined with silk.

Positioning the blocks

A network of lines or a grid of intersecting lines can be used to help position motifs accurately. A simple grid of squares will enable a single motif to be placed in the same position each time, either at the intersections of the lines or within the squares. When repeated, this will build pattern. A bricked grid will build a half-drop pattern. Any geometric grid can be used as a guide for placing motifs, and the lines that form the grid can be straight or curved, regular or distorted.

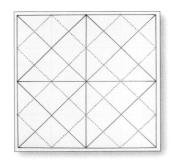

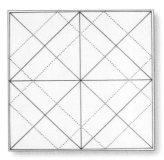

The drawings on the right show how the look of a pattern can vary just by placing the elements that make it up in a different grid.

Straight stitches and detached chain stitches in the complementary colours blue and orange have been used to embellish this formal pattern, which is made up of small elements placed within a grid.

Design possibilities for pattern

When you have a motif for a block that you are happy with, try out different ideas to see how the pattern forms when it is repeated. This could be done by photocopying a drawn image or cutting the shape out from coloured paper. Try some of the ideas listed below.

- Single motifs may be linked together using a line or stripe.
- Place the motif within a grid (a regular network of lines, usually straight but could be curved). The blue and orange design shown on the previous page is a good example of this.
- Create a counterchange effect by reversing the colour or tone in alternate blocks.
- Create a half-drop pattern by placing the motif within a bricked grid.
- Change the scale so that small and large motifs are combined.
- Fill each section of a grid with a different motif. This could be a collection of lines that change with each block or a motif that becomes more or less complex by adding or taking away detail.
- What happens when a secondary motif is added?
- Try cutting part of the pattern away to create a lacy effect.
- Place several motifs one on top of another, attaching them together either through the centre or by one section only. The top one can be folded in half to make it stand away from the one beneath.

Below left: this half-drop pattern was created by printing with a textured roller.

Below right: to create this pattern I have cut part of the pattern away to make a lacy effect and layered it with a coloured background.

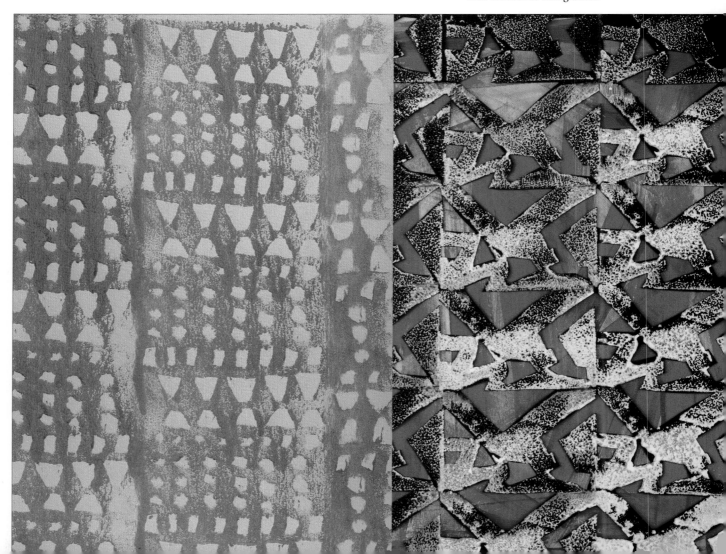

This motif works well in a circular pattern because it narrows to one end, thus making it possible to place it on lines radiating from the centre of a circle. This is the design for the circular bag shown on page 31.

Below left: a secondary motif has been added to the first print to make a more complex image.

Below right: this block has been placed end to end so that the shapes through the middle join up and connect other areas, giving a flow of colour across the pattern.

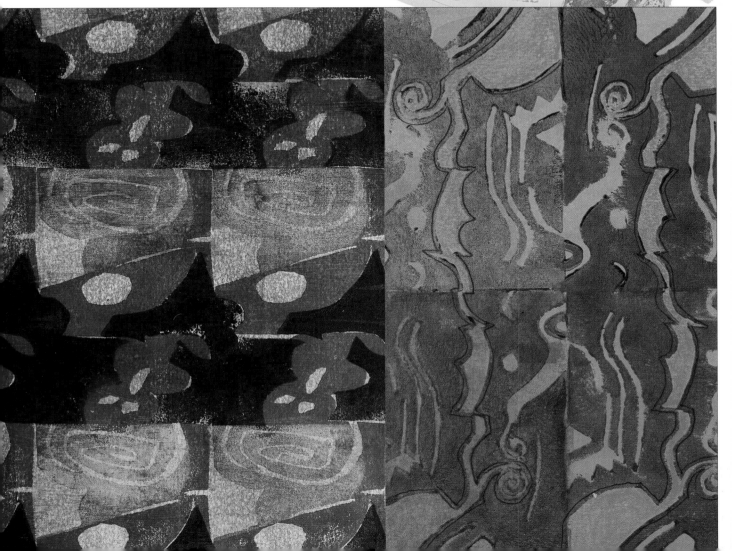

Theme 1: Objects on a shelf

Still-life subjects have been popular for a long time and you do not have to look very far to find images that can be developed for print and stitch. For this exercise, I have chosen part of a shelf with a few pots and plates on it. I have first recorded the image by drawing it. I could also have taken a photograph and made a tracing of the part that interested me, or used a picture from a magazine. You don't have to include every detail. Making a design is about choosing and arranging. The next stage allows you to make those choices and to rearrange parts of the image if you think it is necessary.

I selected part of the shelf that had some contrasting items. I made a pencil drawing of the main shapes, leaving out the pattern on the china. I didn't want anything too fussy or complicated as I knew I could add detail at a later stage.

I drew the image again and darkened the background, as this made the shapes more obvious.

I then drew the image a third time, reducing it to outline shapes against a dark background. I emphasised the divisions at the back of the shelf as they seemed to tie the shapes together. Notice how the shapes overlap each other, making a continuous band. Consider this drawing to be a skeleton so what you need are the 'bones'.

I have experimented with colour to get a feel for how the image would read when printed, and limited the choice here to the complementary colours of blue and orange to give maximum contrast.

A linear drawing will photocopy well, relieving the need to keep redrawing. I have used a photocopy as a template to create a design in cut paper, but as an alternative you could just paint a copy with your chosen colour using acrylics or coloured pencils. Try some different colourways and choose the one that you like the best.

Using magazine papers with a range of blues.

A photocopy painted in blue only. To be able to read the shapes, some of them have a white line around them.

I have explored light, medium and dark tones of blue, with a tiny flash of orange for contrast.

Now I have changed all the foreground shapes to orange and the background shapes to blue.

I have re-created the image using cut paper that I have coloured myself. The main shapes are set against an orange background.

This time I have picked out two shapes in orange with all the others dark blue against a grey-blue background.

Here I decided to pick out one key shape to contrast against white and a blue background.

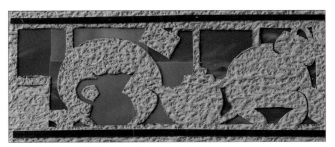

Finally, I made a template from my simplified drawing, enabling me to transfer the image to foam to make the block.

To create the abstract design, I first produced a line drawing with the shapes filled with lines.

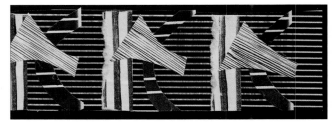

The abstract design uses elements from the original drawing. I have selected the curve of the edge of a plate, a shape hanging across the plate and the vertical divisions of the background. Inspired by the lines of the previous image, I have used lined paper.

Objects-on-a-shelf panel

Several blocks have been used to create a design for a panel. An oblong block cut from Speedy-carve shows the objects on a shelf. The abstract border block is made from soft-cut lino and a separate small jug-shaped block is repeated to create a strip of pattern. The plate motif is printed with a foam circle block. Stitching is a mixture of free machining and hand stitching in a limited colour scheme to texture and enhance the print, continuing my exploration of the complementary colours blue and orange. The stitches used are straight stitch, back stitch and couching and the threads a mixture of cotton, silk and rayon.

Theme 2: Patterned cloth

A piece of cloth from India was the inspiration for a drawing done with
a black fine-liner pen. I placed the fabric in a heap, creating folds and
undulations, as this made sure that I was not going to merely copy the
pattern as it appeared on the cloth. Instead it has given me a fresh pattern,
with details contained within the lines that are created by the folds. This is
a useful method when you want to avoid repeating a pattern exactly.
A photocopy of an image can be scrumpled up and then the creases ironed
in to achieve a similar effect.

*The piece of Indian patterned cloth that
inspired this design.*

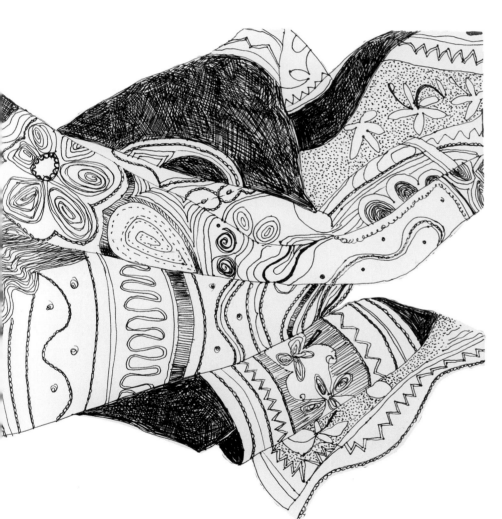

I imposed my own choice of colour on to this new image by redrawing using
chalk pastels. I now have a drawing showing a pattern that is quite different
in style and quality from the one on the original piece of cloth, which has
brightly coloured stitching with strong contrasts on a dark background, and
is very typically Indian.

I made a further drawing using watercolour so that I could add some stitch marks, and this is the one that finally translated into several different blocks. Once again, one detailed drawing has proved very fruitful in terms of inspiration and I have returned to it again and again.

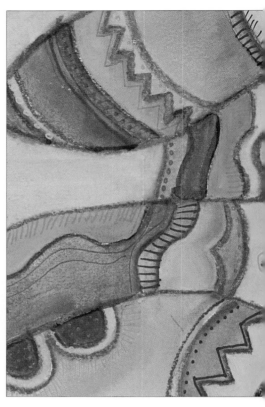

Here are four different prints made from the same lino block. A secondary block has been added to change the colour in the negative spaces. The image shown far right has a texture printed over the first print before adding a further print, creating plain and textured areas within the image.

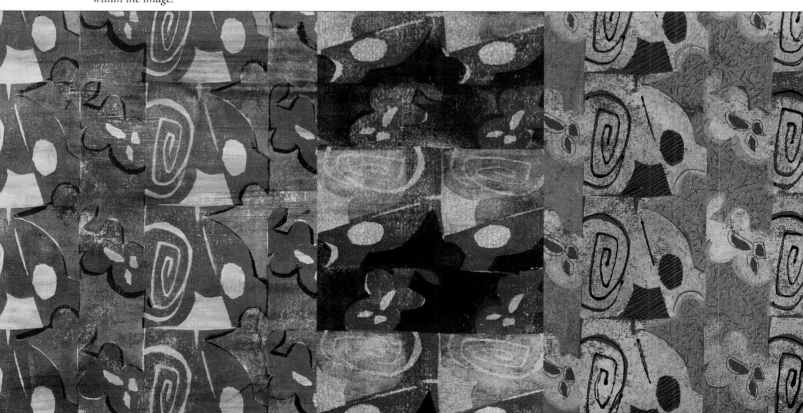

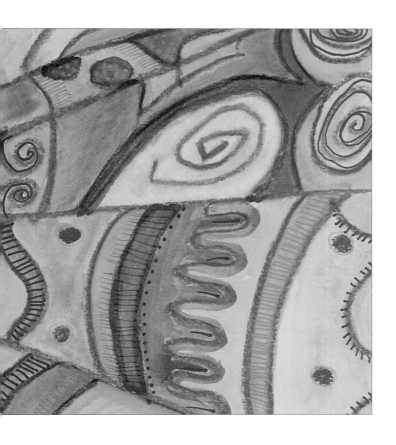

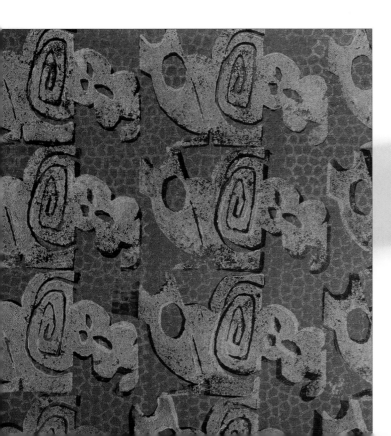

Vessel

Dyed cotton fabric was first printed with a texture block and over-printed with a relief block. A second print in a different colour gives a dark ghosting around the shape. The resulting fabric is decorated with hand stitching to create a surface texture. The stitches used are seeding, couching and blocks of satin stitch in the background. The finished textile is stretched over a strong card tube to make a vessel and lined with felt. The lid is printed with a texture block and hand stitched with blocks of satin stitch.

Theme 3: Rock carving

A holiday in Northern Cyprus was the inspiration for this interpretation into print. The drawing was made at the ancient site of Salamis using a soft pencil. Various pieces of broken, carved architecture lay strewn on the ground just waiting for me to come along and see the potential for translation into a textile.

I was drawn to the tonal effects of the carved surface and the spirals within it. Several separate motifs were developed from the drawing, each one giving the criteria required for a successful motif, that is, contrast of mass and of positive versus negative space.

I have used the image for templates and stencils as well as for print.

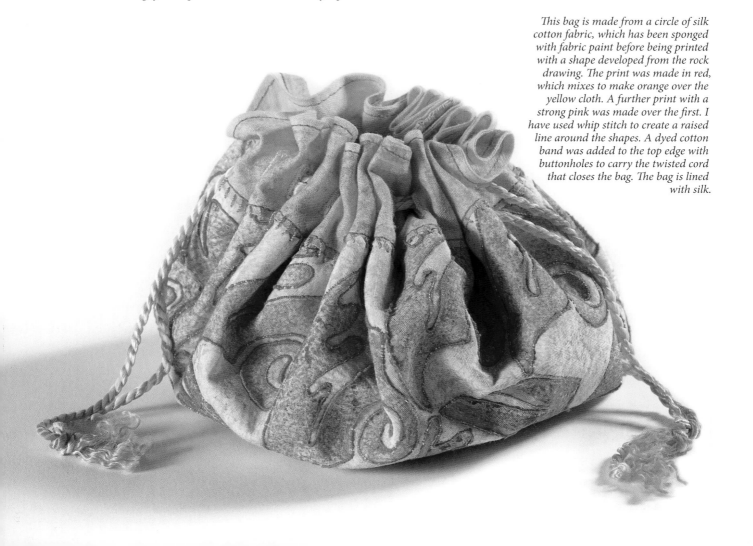

This bag is made from a circle of silk cotton fabric, which has been sponged with fabric paint before being printed with a shape developed from the rock drawing. The print was made in red, which mixes to make orange over the yellow cloth. A further print with a strong pink was made over the first. I have used whip stitch to create a raised line around the shapes. A dyed cotton band was added to the top edge with buttonholes to carry the twisted cord that closes the bag. The bag is lined with silk.

Theme 4: Beetles

I first saw these beetles on a greetings card and recognised their potential as a design source. I went to the library and found a book in the children's section that showed very clear images of a number of insects. I made some drawings of them and worked in black and white to create several ideas using cut paper. This method helped to simplify the images and gave me lots of ways that I could put them together to make pattern. I have used a number of design methods to generate the ideas: counterchange, changing the scale, combining two different images and changing the direction of some of them. If you are not sure how to use a motif, it is always worth taking the time to play with ideas first without trying to decide what to do in your head. Have a go and see what emerges.

Notice that the motifs I have used have a solid body and contrasting fine details for legs, head and feelers, which provides the ideal contrast for a good motif. The potential with this motif has yielded some rich pattern with great ideas for stitch.

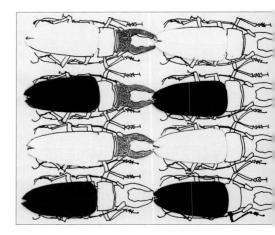

Making a drawing on to tracing paper meant that I could easily photocopy it, change the scale and cut and piece motifs together to build the pattern.

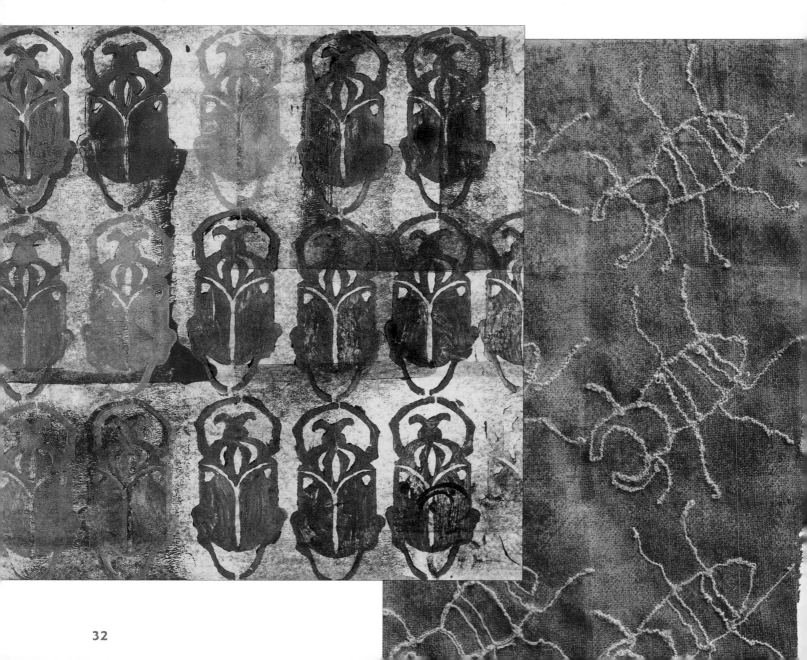

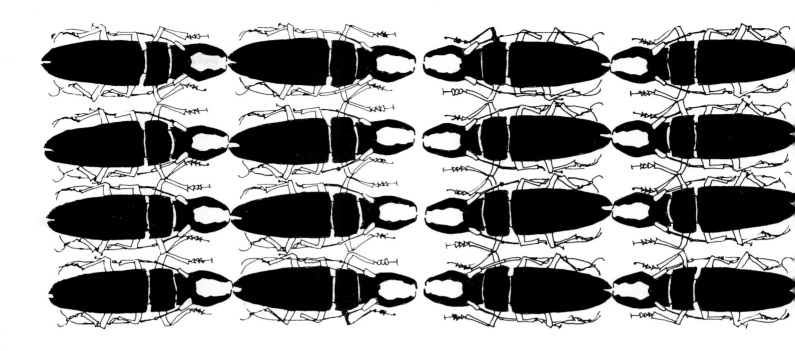

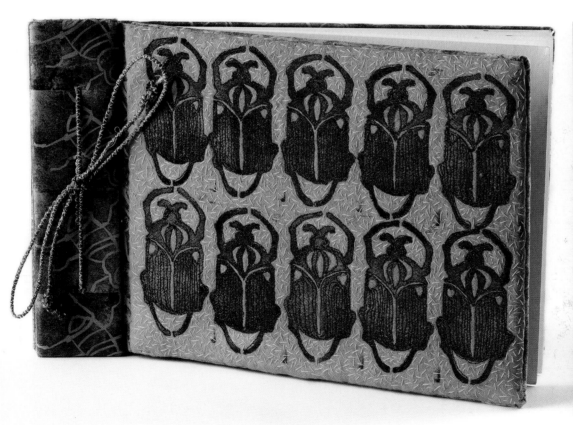

Beetle book

This is a simple handmade book form with the cover decorated using a design developed from beetles. The design was cut into an eraser block and printed on to dyed fabric. The pattern is embellished with free machining using a variegated metallic thread, and seeding is added to the background. The inside lining of the book (see the detail, right) is printed with a different eraser block on to a glazed cotton fabric, creating an all-over pattern. The book is held together with a machine-made cord.

Theme 5: Guatemala

Looking at the textiles from Guatemala has been a rich experience in design terms. There is vibrant colour, with hot reds, orange, pink, green, blue and yellow, woven together to give a vivid palette. Simple geometric shape combines with floral imagery dotted about with stylised birds and animals. Working with such an exciting vocabulary has produced lots of ideas for design and stitch.

I have used waxed papers and fabrics and combined them with simple stitch. Working with strips to reflect the weaving techniques of this area of the world, the work was layered, first making waxed papers to join in strips. I then cut triangles and diamond shapes to apply with glue in the first instance and then added stitch. I re-waxed the designs to push the stitching into the surface so that it would read as marks to complement the whole.

I developed a print block of a turkey and a bird and used them to print papers and fabric. I cut them out and applied them to the geometric patterns that I have created.

I also used a wooden block that I had in my collection of a stylised figure that seems to fit with the other imagery found on the Guatemalan textiles.

This journey has been a very satisfying exploration of Guatemalan textiles that has a lot more to offer when time permits.

The design above uses waxed papers with diamonds and triangles placed in strips to reflect the strip weaving that is typical of Guatemalan textiles. Prints of a turkey motif have been cut out and applied with straight stitch. The piece was re-waxed and ironed to push the stitching into the surface and to remove surplus wax.

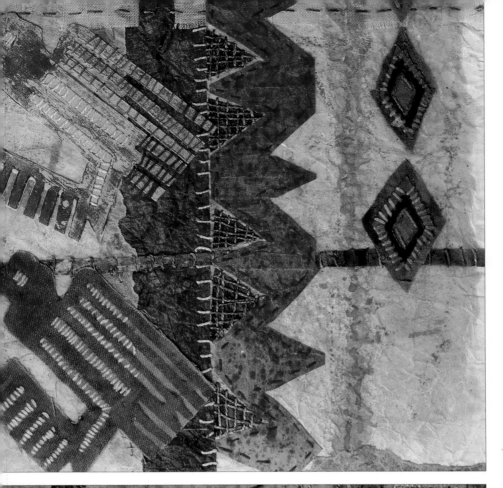

Leather-covered book

The leather cover for the handmade book shown above is printed with a block developed from a motif found on a Guatemalan textile. The print is outlined with free machine stitching. A single motif stitched on to a dissolvable background is applied to the print.

All these designs reflect the characteristics of Guatemalan textiles: the bright primary colours, the geometric shapes and stylised birds.

Colour

Colour can be a very personal experience. We all react to it and are affected by colour in a very individual way, and have our favourite colours and ones that we do not like. We experience colour mainly through our eyes but also through our emotions, consciously and unconsciously. Our language is so littered with references to colour that it is obvious that it is an integral part of our lives, even if we have not acknowledged the

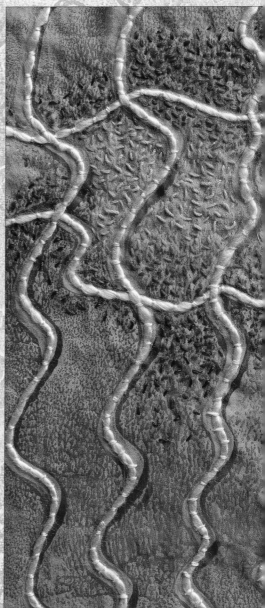

Above: a monoprint is decorated with couching and seeding.

Left: a cool colour scheme of greens and blues is stitched by machine on to a soft-cut lino print. The resulting fabric has been cut up and applied to another piece of fabric printed with a texture block. Further stitching is added by hand.

This shows a warm colour scheme using reds, yellows, oranges and pinks to texture the monoprinted surface with buttonhole stitch.

fact. Consider phrases like 'feeling blue' or 'seeing red', being 'in the red', 'purple with rage', or 'green with envy'. Colour symbolism is another dimension of colour that varies from culture to culture around the world.

Although we experience colour every day through feeling and seeing, and through understanding the symbols, it is useful to have some understanding of the principles of colour when involved in creative work. Knowing what colours work well together and how to select a particular colour scheme for a specific mood or effect is a great help.

There are numerous excellent books available that deal with colour. Many are very detailed in their approach but are often too technical for the average user. For the most part, it is enough to know the basics of primary, secondary and tertiary colours together with tints and shades; how they are arranged in a simple colour wheel; and how to select a suitable and effective colour palette to satisfy an individual need.

When more detailed knowledge is required, working through colour exercises and practising with mixing paint will provide further experience of the differences between, and the effects of, pigments, surfaces and colour densities.

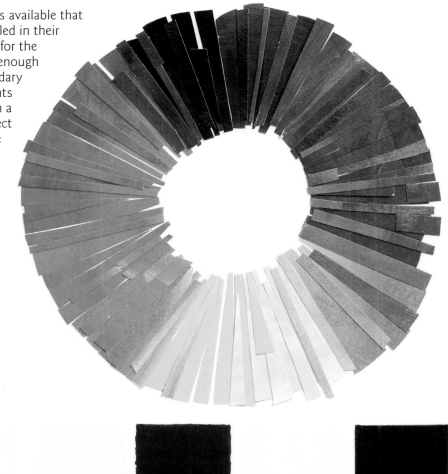

Right: a colour wheel made from cut strips of paper.

Below: useful colour exercises include mixing colours with more and more white to make tints or black to make shades.

There are three primary colours: red, blue and yellow. When two primaries are mixed together, secondary colours are made. Red mixed with blue makes purple, blue mixed with yellow makes green, and red mixed with yellow gives orange. The tertiary colours, or intermediate colours, are yellow-orange, yellow-green, red-purple, red-orange, blue-green and blue-purple. Each contains a mix of a primary with a secondary. All of this makes much more sense when seen as a circle of colour, gradually moving from one to another.

The primary colours, red, blue and yellow, give a bright, colourful effect. Here, a collagraph print was made on to yellow silk and embellished with buttonhole and running stitch in all three colours.

A soft-cut lino print is decorated with cretan stitch and couching using the three secondary colours, purple, green and orange.

Complementary colours, yellow and purple, have been used to create this sample. A purple print was made on to yellow cotton with a block made from Speedy-carve. Most of the print is left plain but the background is textured with chain stitch, the jug with purple chain stitch and the frame with running stitch.

Tints are made by mixing a colour with white, creating pale colours; shades are a mixture of a colour with black, resulting in dark colours. Wonderful subtle mixes of colour can be achieved by mixing one colour of paint through to another in ten stages or more. This can also be done by over-printing to mix the colour, or by stitching and optically mixing the colour, as shown opposite.

We generally find it difficult to visualise the many subtle colours that can be obtained by mixing either black to white or a primary or secondary colour to another in stages. For instance, if you take white and add tiny amounts of another colour to it, a range of soft, pale colours can be achieved. By mixing very small amounts of black to a colour, you will have a range of dark colours. It is useful, when selecting colours, to be able to see these in front of you on the page. This exercise also gives valuable practice in mixing paint so that you get better at knowing which pigments go together to make specific colours, tints and shades.

Above: a potato print on cotton fabric was stitched by hand using couching and straight stitches. The colour is muted and neutral and is an example of tints; that is, colour with white added.

Left: a soft-cut lino block was printed on to calico and free machined in tones of white, black and grey.

PRINTING

As a means of adding colour and visual texture to the surface of fabric, print offers a wide palette of easily accessible methods, from the painterly qualities of monoprint to the precise registration of repeat pattern and the satisfaction of recycling found objects to create new images. The ability to build pattern relatively quickly is an advantage and very subtle mixes of colour can be achieved by over-printing, dark on light, light on dark, bright colour to enliven and tertiary mixes to dull down.

There are so many methods of arriving at a print that, if you are a beginner, it can be rather confusing to know where to start. Each method has its own characteristic result, and until experience is gained, it can be difficult to make a choice. With practice, you will come to know what kind of mark you want to make, or what kind of image you are planning, and that can help you to choose which technique will best give you what you are looking for. Most of the methods that are described in this book are relatively simple ones, using materials that are readily available and, in many cases, recycled.

Making a print on to paper is a little easier than making it on to fabric. I use cheap paper for trying out a block, or make the prints directly into my sketchbook. I try out patterns and combinations first to help me make decisions about how I want to use the print on fabric.

Left: collagraph prints using squares and circles are explored in my sketchbook.

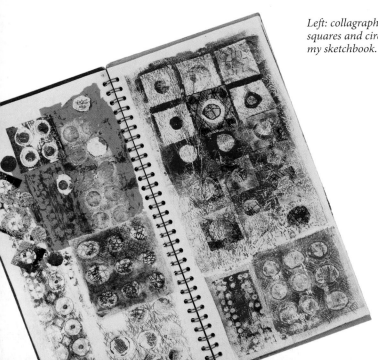

Right: a card block is printed over torn paper strips that have been applied to a painted page.

Far right: a variety of prints made on paper using relief blocks, eraser blocks, potato prints and monoprinting.

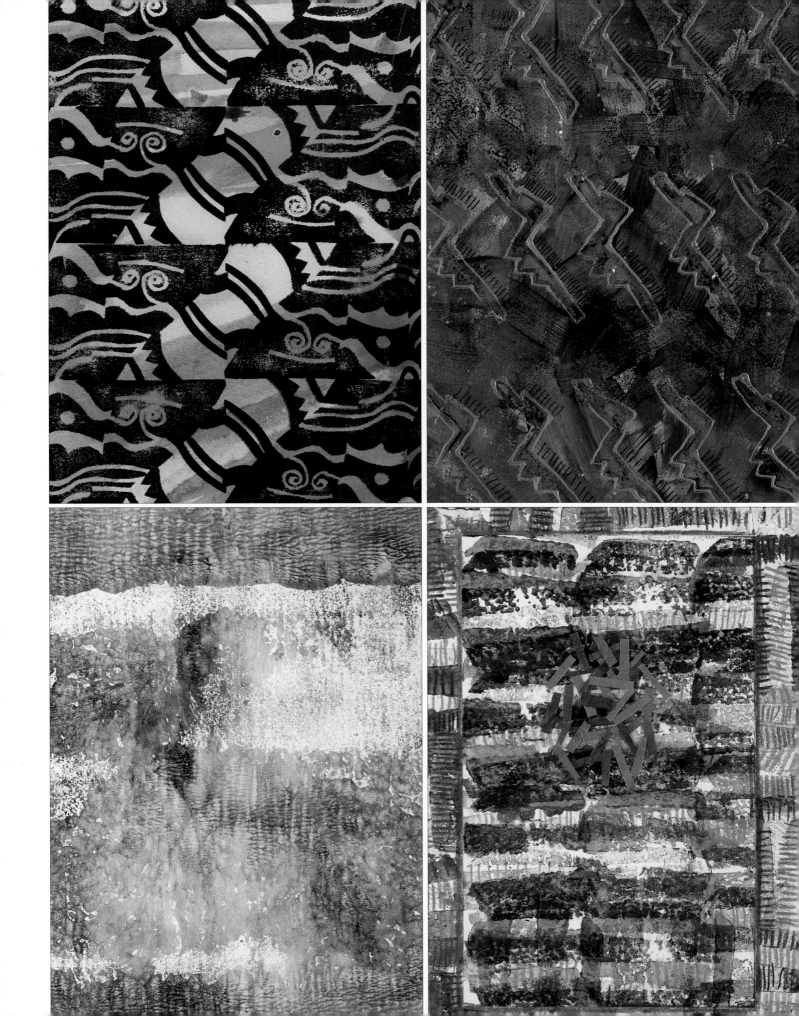

Why print, which print?

Printing is a reliable and simple method of transferring designs to either paper or fabric, but it can be made so much more exciting. Texture, pattern, subtle mixes of stippled colour, painterly effects and linear images can all be achieved using print. It can be a way of applying a texture to fabric, altering the colour very subtly, or making a definite contrast in colour or tone.

Its great strength is in building pattern. The ability to reproduce an exact image again and again quickly makes it ideal for pattern. With one simple shape, infinite patterns and variations can be achieved. By understanding the underlying structure of a formal pattern, intricate patterned surfaces can be built by placing the motif in key positions. Multiple shapes and images can be combined, tessellated or over-printed to produce intriguing and exciting surfaces ready for stitching.

If texture is required, a textured roller or a texture block can be used to print on to fabric before further prints are made on top. The inking up of the block can give texture if the paint is applied unevenly or loosely with a brush or sponge.

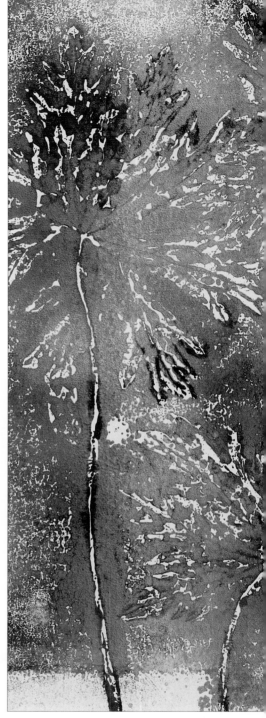

A leaf was used as a resist for this monoprint.

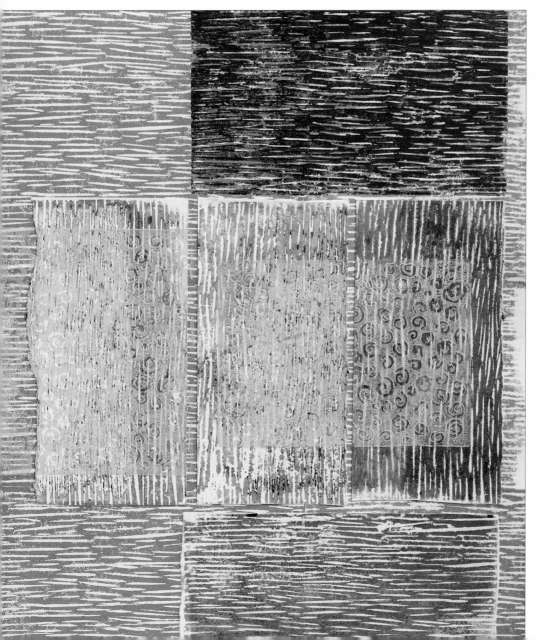

A texture block was repeat printed, making a background, with some over-printing. A further block was printed over the top in yellow to create an abstract design.

Knowledge and experience of the various methods at your disposal are essential. Being able to choose an appropriate technique, which will give you the type of mark to express the mood or serve the end result that you want, will save you time and hours of frustration. A summary of the characteristics of each technique are given here to enable you to select the best method for your purpose.

Block print
Crisp, clear edges; good for repeating shapes; blocks may disintegrate if over used.

Eraser print
Few tools needed; durable; washable; easy to cut; design can be drawn on to the surface; gives good, clear print even when relatively dry.

Monoprint
Painterly effects; good for resists, line, texture; mixing colour in same print; only one or two prints can be made.

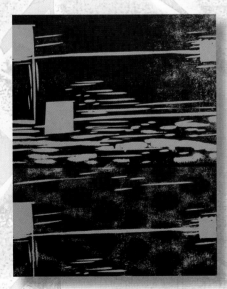

Lino print
Needs specialist cutting tools; good for intricate designs; works best with a press but not essential; good, clear marks/ edges; interesting textures can result from cut areas.

Collagraph
Good for background texture; gives opportunity to recycle materials so is economical; size is limited without a press but works well with burnishing.

Found objects
Not all take ink very well so a fabric medium is needed; unusual and surprising effects can often be obtained.

Block printing

Blocks for printing, sometimes described as relief blocks, can be made from a variety of materials, including card, plastic and wood. Lino is also commonly used in print, but there are some good alternatives to this material.

Blocks can be used singly, to give an individual spot motif or to build a repeat pattern, or several blocks can be set together to create a more complex image. Multiple blocks may be equal in size and shape or may tessellate or combine, as in a jigsaw. Each one can also be completely different in shape. Interlocking jigsaw blocks, symmetrical or irregular, provide an opportunity to explore colour: each block can have a different colour, relieving the need to clean a block each time the colour is changed. When working with blocks in this way, careful registration is essential for the building of the image.

Cleaning up

It is not a good idea to let paint or ink dry on a block, whatever it is made of. Dry ink will clog the detail of your block and could leave an uneven surface that will pick up unevenly when further prints are taken. Wipe card blocks with a damp sponge and then quickly run them under the tap to remove the rest of the paint, if necessary. Prolonged wetting will cause them to buckle and disintegrate. Blot them dry with a paper towel and leave them to dry completely. I put mine in the airing cupboard. Plastic erasers can simply be washed off under a running tap and dried with a paper towel.

A selection of card blocks for printing.

Making card and foam blocks

These can be made from off-cuts of mount card or with thin foam sheets, as shown in these instructions. Transfer the image to the foam using a tracing method or by drawing around a shape. The motif can be cut with a craft knife or with scissors (see the instructions below), making sure that any holes are not too small and that acute angles are rounded off, as otherwise they will become clogged with ink or paint.

Work with a craft knife on a cutting mat, making sure that your fingers are always behind the cutting edge and that you cut away from the body when cutting card. Don't expect the knife to cut through the first time you draw it over the card. It will take several strokes of the knife to cut through completely, depending on the thickness of the card. Another tip is to work with a sharp blade. It can be frustrating trying to cut through card when the blade is blunt, as you may tear the card and you will be more likely to cut yourself. Also, more pressure is needed which can put undue strain on your fingers and wrists. It is easier to work standing up as the downward pressure is a more efficient way of using your effort.

Ideally, the motif will sit on top of the background card, with its edges matching or touching the edges of the background. Avoid having a motif sitting in the middle of a piece of card with a lot of space around it – the surrounding space will fill with unwanted ink, and it will be difficult to register the design when printing. You need to know where the edge of the motif is when a print is made.

Making a block

Begin by drawing your chosen design on to paper.

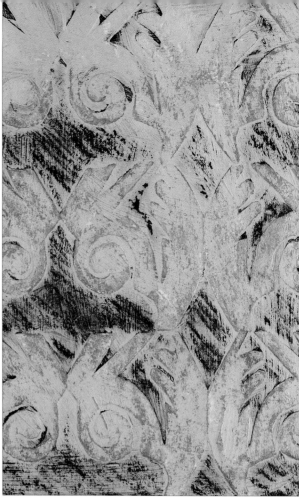

A design developed from a drawing of carved stone (see page 30). The print was cut out and applied to paper with colour and drawing added on top.

1 Working on a craft mat, trace the design on to tracing paper using a sharp, soft (2B or 3B) pencil.

2 Turn the tracing over and draw over all the lines accurately and firmly.

MATERIALS

- Drawing or photocopy of a motif
- Tracing paper and soft pencil (2B or 3B)
- Small piece of Funky Foam or mount card
- Small piece of card
- Strong PVA glue
- Craft knife, small, sharp scissors and a metal ruler
- Cutting mat or piece of thick board to protect your table surface
- Button polish
- Old, stiff paintbrush
- Small piece of paper (optional)
- Masking tape (optional)

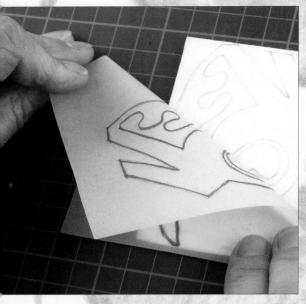

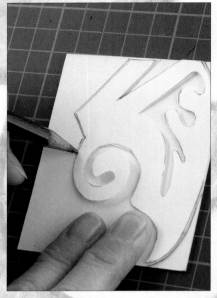

Tip

To avoid surplus paint on the negative areas of the block, make sure the edges of the shape fit right up to the edge of the foam or card. You may wish to cut away the surrounding card.

3 Turn the tracing back over so that it is face up, place it on the piece of foam and draw firmly over the outline. The design should now be transferred to the foam.

An alternative method for transferring the design on to the foam or card is to cut out the paper shape to make a template, then draw round the shape on to the foam or card.

Tip

If you have internal spaces to cut, use a scalpel rather than scissors as this is easier to get into the corners.

4 Cut out the design using a pair of small, sharp scissors.

5 Cut out the internal areas with a craft knife.

6 Cover the back of the design with strong PVA glue using an old, stiff paintbrush. Make sure it is evenly covered, right up to the edges.

7 Press the design down firmly on to the piece of card and allow to dry. Make sure the edges of the design match the edges of the card. Trim the card to fit, if necessary.

8 Wearing protective gloves, seal the back of the card with button polish. This prevents the card from disintegrating when it gets wet.

9 Turn the block over and seal in between the foam shape. Leave the block to dry overnight.

Tip

If your design is cut from card, seal the block all over, including the design.

10 I usually add a small tab to the back of the block, made from a piece of folded paper and secured with masking tape. This is particularly important if the block is small. It enables me to lift the block from the printed surface more easily and removes the problem of dirty fingers transferring unwanted paint to the paper or fabric as the block is lifted. In addition, mark the back of the block with an arrow to indicate the top, as you won't be able to see which way up it is when you are printing. It is a good idea, too, to mark any point which needs to line up with successive prints.

A completed and used block. Notice that the surrounding area is cut away.

Printing on paper

Once your block is complete it is ready for inking up. Try it on paper first, working with acrylics mixed with a small amount of fabric medium to give you a longer working time and a sticky consistency. I would advise against using the cheap acrylic paint that is available in DIY stores. It is often very runny and the colours are not very good. Use a recognised brand and it should serve you well. You could use block-printing ink if you wish as it is designed for the job and you don't then have to add medium to it.

You will need a smooth, flat surface to work on as any undulations or lumps or bumps will be transferred to your print. I use a piece of glass or acrylic sheet. Protect your hands and clothes by wearing protective gloves and either an apron or overall.

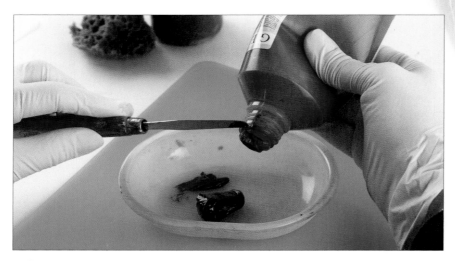

1 Put some acrylic paint into the palette with a palette knife or small plastic spoon, remembering to wipe the knife clean afterwards. If necessary, add a second colour and mix them together with the palette knife to get the exact colour you want.

MATERIALS

Water-based printing ink or acrylic paint

Small plastic pot for use as a palette

Palette knife or small plastic spoon

Piece of glass or acrylic sheet (printing plate)

Piece of blanket or foam mouse mat

Paper to print on

Small piece of sponge

Protective gloves and overall or apron

Paper towel

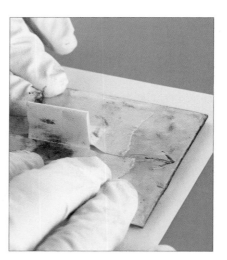

2 Lay the paper on the printing plate. Dip a small piece of sponge into the paint and apply it evenly to the block using a dabbing action rather than wiping the ink on.

3 When the block is completely covered with paint, place it paint-side down firmly on to the paper. Press firmly and evenly on to the back of the block.

Tip

You will find that the way a block is inked up can make a difference to the resulting print. Any unevenness in applying the ink will show in the print. If a hard bristle brush is used to apply the ink, you may see the streaks in the print. A soft brush may take off as much ink as it puts on.

Take care not to overload the block with paint as any surplus will ooze out around the edges of the block or into areas where you don't want it to go. Having said that, you need enough paint, evenly spread, to get a good print.

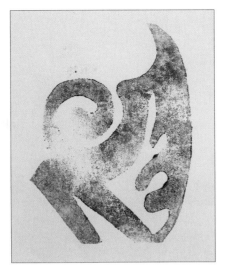

 Lift the block away to reveal the print.

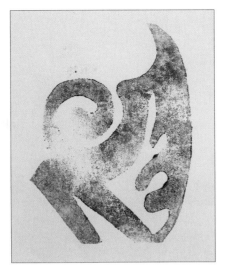 Now is the time to make any adjustment to the amount of paint used to ink up the block. If the print is thin and patchy, like the one shown above, it will need more paint.

 If detail has filled with paint and spread out beyond the edges of the shape, there was probably too much paint on the block and less next time should improve the impression.

Tip

Don't worry if each print varies from the one before. One of the characteristics of repeat printing is that there is variety in the amount of ink that is transferred each time.

 To create a repeat pattern, ink the block again and align it with the previous print, using the marks made on the back of the block (see step 10 on page 49).

 Lift off the block, revealing the print underneath.

Tip

Careful registration is needed for the second print if you want the pattern to join up. Make sure any marks are lined up and that the block is the right way up if that is important.

Printing on fabric

You will need the same smooth, flat surface as for printing on paper. It helps to have a slightly soft surface so that the block is pressed into the fabric. Ink or paint may well pass right through the fabric so it is best if your print area is also wipeable. I use a piece of table protector which has a foam backing and I can wipe the surface clean, if necessary.

When you are happy with the print, try it on fabric, using fabric paint or screen-printing ink. I often use acrylics on fabric but it does make the fabric rather stiff and not so comfortable to stitch into. If the end result is to be worn or handled a lot, I would prefer to print with fabric paint, which is, after all, designed for fabric. Fabric paint is more liquid than acrylic paint and will soak into the fabric much more readily. Test it first, as the consistency will vary from brand to brand and fabric to fabric. Wear protective gloves and clothing, as before.

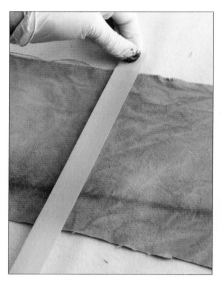

1 Mix the fabric paint in a plastic palette (see page 50) and cover your worksurface with a padded table covering. Tape your washed, ironed fabric to the print surface with masking tape. The fabric will stick to the block otherwise and this may spoil the print.

2 Ink up the block as before, using a sponge. Remove any excess that is trapped in the small gaps with a palette knife.

Tip

Remember that the paint should be sticky rather than wet. If it is too wet, the paint will bleed into the fabric, blurring the edges of the image. It takes practice to get this right so don't despair if you don't get it right the first time you try it. Different brands of paint have different consistencies, and the age of the paint makes a difference too, so it is difficult to give exact proportions of paint to medium.

3 Press the block down firmly and evenly on the fabric.

4 Lift off the block with a smooth, confident movement, revealing the design underneath.

Tip

Clean the block with paper towel after use, or to remove any excess between prints.

5 Repeat the design several times to create a pattern on the fabric. Do not be too concerned about some unevenness in the prints, nor about any extraneous marks that might appear outside the design – this all adds to the character of the piece.

6 The print should be heat fixed when it is dry. Follow the manufacturer's instructions on the jar of paint for temperature and length of time to heat it. Protect your iron and ironing surface with baking parchment or calico to prevent any transfer of paint.

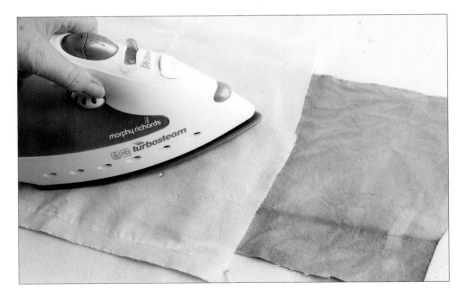

Over-printing

Over-printing is a way of achieving a more complex image, or of blending and mixing colour. It is a good idea to begin with lighter colours and let them dry before placing the same print over the top. It is very difficult to place it exactly over the first print but what you are aiming for is a shadow effect with the first print showing around the edges of the second one. Many layers can be added, though remember to allow the paint to dry in between.

You could try printing with a texture first. One with small, closely spaced marks will usually work better than one that conflicts with the pattern to be printed over the top. When the first layer of paint is dry, try over-printing with a lighter colour on to dark or dark on to light. Explore colour relationships by combining strong colours, or contrast light and dark colours. Another variation is to print on to coloured paper, which will change your printed colour, and more colour could be printed over the top.

Tip
Try drawing on to the print with felt-tip or gel pens, or use glitter to enhance the design.

2 Lay the block over the first image, press down firmly and lift off. There is no need to be too accurate — you can get a more interesting result if the second print is not exactly aligned with the first. Some of the first colour will show through, but again this improves the overall design.

1 Mix the second colour in a clean dish and dab it on to the block with a sponge, as before.

3 Repeat the process on the remaining images and heat fix, as described on page 53.

Here, the paper has been coloured using a textured roller before over-printing with a foam block.

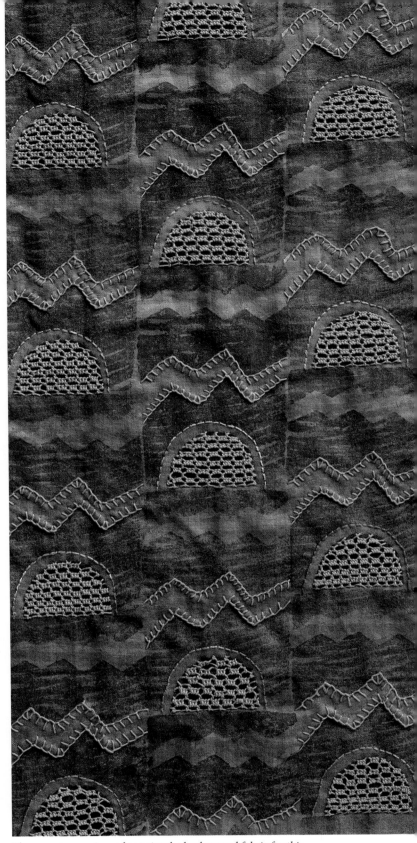

The same process is used to print the background fabric for this stitched sample. Dyed cotton fabric was textured with a roller and over-printed with a foam block. Using cotton perle thread, a buttonhole edging creates bands that contrast with the domed shapes. These are filled with triple Brussels stitch – a needlelace stitch that is a variation of buttonhole stitch. The printed fabric would be suitable for making a small bag or book cover.

Origami box

I liked the challenge of making an origami box using folded fabric. The choice of fabric is important as it will be folded a number of times and too much bulk will distort the shape. Fine, closely woven cottons such as lawn or fine calico work well, as does cotton organdie.

Calico takes a good crease but the shape still needed a lid to keep it true and a base made from covered card adds to the stability.

I tested the folded shape in paper first so that I could see where the print should be. When folding the shape, some of the design is on one side of the paper and some on the reverse. I designed a relief block that exactly fits the shape and printed with acrylic paint in sections of the fabric where required. The design was embellished with free machining using a variegated thread. The stitching had to be as good on the reverse side of the fabric as on the top as both sides would be visible.

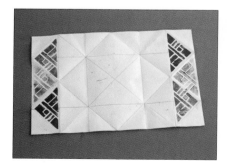

1 First fold sheet of paper, following the steps which follow, to indicate where to place the print, then print the outer sections.

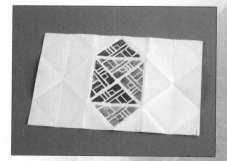

2 Turn the paper over and print the middle square and upper and lower triangles, as shown.

3 Turn the paper back over again and fold it into thirds, with the outer sections folded back on to themselves.

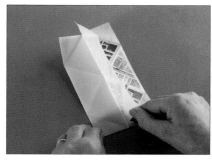

4 Fold the left-hand flap back over to the right.

5 Fold down the four corners to make a point at each end.

6 Fold the left-hand flap back on itself, then fold the right-hand flap over to the left.

7 Fold down the four corners as in step 5. Fold the right-hand flap back on itself, revealing the patterned edges.

8 When folded to this stage the print should show on the front and on the back.

9 Turn the paper back over and, pulling from the centre outwards and re-creasing, open up the shape to create a box.

I have added lids, bases and feet to these boxes. The lids have various types of knobs. For the purple and yellow box, I have developed a knob using the unit shape, which is a triangle. Rolled and folded paper were used for the others.

Eraser blocks

Plastic pencil erasers are cheap and easy to acquire from stationery suppliers. They are ideal for making detailed blocks as they are easy to cut. It feels rather like cutting through cheese when cutting into an eraser block. Erasers can be divided into smaller pieces for tiny images without fear of them disintegrating, or set together if a larger image is needed. The thickness of erasers means that you can cut a design into both sides, making them very economical. They are also easy to clean. Just run them under cold water to wash off the paint and dry with a paper towel.

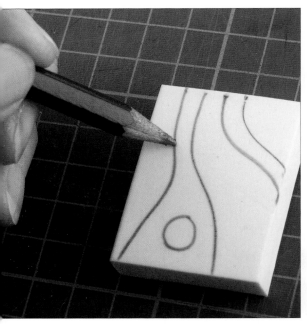

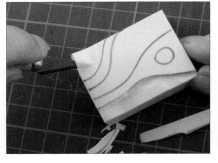

1 Mark the design directly on to the eraser using either a pencil or a ballpoint pen. Alternatively, transfer it from a drawing. Choose a design that is suitable for the scale of the eraser, keeping it simple, without too much detail. Decide in advance which parts of the design are to be cut away and mark these, if necessary.

2 Work with a scalpel that has a sharp, pointed blade, and cut into the plastic, holding the knife at a slight angle. Aim to cut away the surface down to about 2mm (¹⁄₁₆in) depth, clearing away any tiny crumbs of plastic that may wedge themselves into the cuts.

3 When cutting along a thin line, angle the knife along the line on one side and repeat on the other, thus cutting a V shape.

4 The plastic should lift out cleanly. Try to avoid cutting into the eraser in such a way that it results in a crumbled surface.

5 Cut out the remaining shapes and add some texture, as desired, to complete the block.

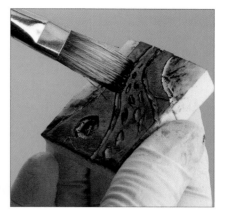

6 Ink up the block using either a small sponge or a stiff paintbrush (a brush is better for smaller blocks with more intricate designs).

7 Print the design on to paper as before, re-inking between each print, or between every other print.

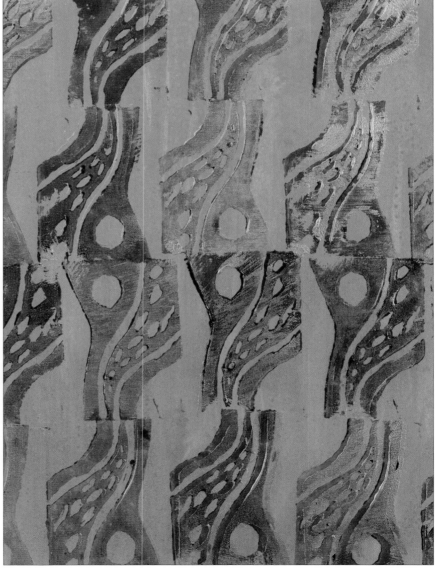

8 If you wish, over-print the design with a different coloured paint. Here I have used a gold metallic paint. This is softer and wetter than fabric paint, so the brush marks will show through the print.

Lino and soft-cut lino printing

The characteristics of lino prints are strong, bold marks. Lino and soft-cut lino prints are good for line and texture, as cut areas bring extra vibrancy. Often used as single images, they can be cut to any particular shape.

Adigraf is very popular in schools. It is green in colour and about 3mm (⅛in) thick. It can be cut into smaller pieces or specific shapes with scissors or with a craft knife. It is a soft acrylic, slightly rubbery to the feel and is very easy to cut with simple lino-cutting tools.

Japanese vinyl is double sided and about the same thickness as Adigraf. It is firmer to handle and has a smooth cutting surface. It is blue on one side and green on the reverse.

Speedy-carve is another similar product but is slightly thicker, enabling designs to be cut on both sides provided that the cuts are not too deep. It is pink in colour and although only available to the trade, it can be found in outlets specialising in art and design products. It is more expensive than the other types.

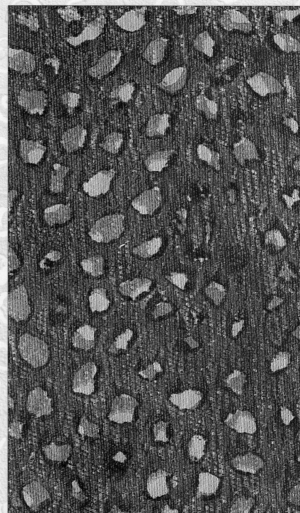

Lino has a long history dating back to the 1860s when linoleum was developed as a flooring medium. Lino prints were made by Russian artists for political posters and by major artists like Picasso and Matisse, creating bold linear and textured images. Prints are made either by using a press or by burnishing with a baren or the back of a spoon.

The surface of the lino should be lightly sanded before using as it has a slightly rough surface. This will make it easier to mark the design and subsequently print. Lino can be more difficult to cut when it is cold but placing it on a warm radiator for a few minutes should soften it sufficiently.

Lino continues to be a popular medium but recently vinyls are being introduced and these are the sort used here. There are a number of types available under a variety of trade names but the key feature of the new material is that it is flexible and much easier to cut into than the traditional linoleum. They are relatively inexpensive and the ones that I have used are Adigraf, Japanese vinyl, and Speedy-carve, all sourced on the internet and available through well-known suppliers.

As usual, prepare your working area with a protective covering that is wipeable and non-slip if you are using traditional lino. When printing on to fabric, place a piece of blanket or foam-backed table protector under it so that there is some 'give' when printing. Prepare the fabric paint by mixing with a fabric medium to thicken it, if necessary. Use a roller if the block is large or a sponge if it is relatively small.

Cutting the lino

You will need a set of lino-cutting tools for this technique. I use a set that is more expensive than the basic set available. Because I do quite a lot of lino cutting, I wanted better quality tools as they are more comfortable to work with, though they do need to be sharpened every so often. They come in a storage box for safety. The basic tools (shown on page 15) are perfectly adequate for the job, and a wooden or plastic handle and a variety of cutters will not cost a lot. New cutters can be bought when they blunt, but they do last a long time if you only do a small amount of work with them.

A set of good quality lino-cutting tools.

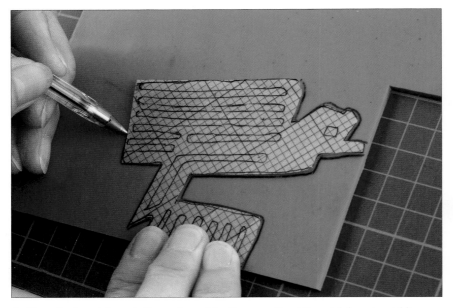

1 Place the template on to the surface of the lino or soft-cut lino and draw around it using a pencil or a ballpoint pen. Remember to consider which way round you want the image to read and reverse the template if you need to. This is especially important if you have text in the design.

MATERIALS

Lino or soft-cut lino, e.g. Adigraf

Carbon paper or tracing paper (optional)

Pencil or ballpoint pen

Lino-cutting tools

2 Remove the template and draw the inner parts of the design freehand.

Alternatively, trace the image on to tracing paper, draw along the lines on the back of the tracing (see page 47), then place the design on the lino or soft-cut lino and trace over the outline again to transfer the image. Carbon paper can also be used.

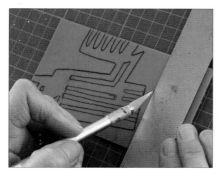

3 Cut the block to the desired size or shape using a craft knife. Align the lino or soft-cut lino with the grid on the cutting mat to ensure the sides are straight, and use the ruler and scalpel to cut away the excess. The edges of the design should touch the sides of the lino.

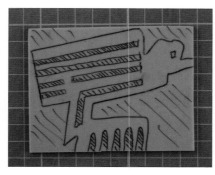

4 Mark which parts of the design are to be cut away.

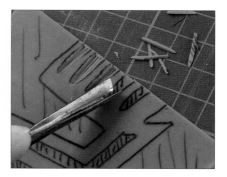

5 Start by using the V-shaped cutting tool to cut away the narrow parts of the design.

6 Change to the U-shaped tool to open up the edge of each of the narrow shapes.

7 Revert to the V-shaped tool for the rest of the lines. Turn the block as you work so you are always pushing the cutting tool away from you.

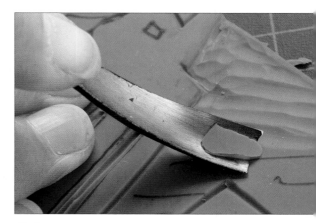

8 Go round the edges of the larger shapes using the V-shaped tool, then change to a broader tool and scoop out the inner parts. Here I have left a ridged surface to create texture. For a smoother finish, continue until the cut-away surface is flat.

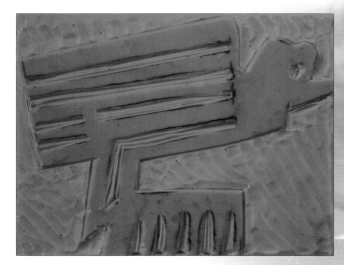

The completed block.

Tip
To create a smooth finish, use foam rather than lino and cut out the positive shape if you do not want to have textural marks around it.

Printing with lino blocks

Soft-cut lino will consistently give good prints and, because it is a flexible material and can be printed around a surface that is curved, I have used it to decorate wooden boxes that often have curved lids. As the blocks are often larger than card blocks, I prefer to ink up with a roller to get an even covering and I have a spare clean roller to add pressure on to the back of the block when taking the print.

Printing on paper

MATERIALS

Soft-cut lino block, e.g. Adigraf
Water-soluble printing inks or fabric paint
Paper or washed, ironed fabric to print on
Masking tape
Roller
Piece of glass or acrylic (plate)
Paper towel for cleaning up
Protective gloves and apron
Iron and board

1 Squeeze a fairly large quantity of ink on to the piece of glass or other smooth surface (the plate). Mix in a second colour if you wish. Here I have added white to blue to make a paler blue.

2 Roll the roller in different directions several times over the ink until there is a thin coat of ink on the roller. Scrape any excess to one side as you work.

3 Roll the inked roller back and forth over the lino block several times until it is coated evenly.

4 Lay the block face down on the paper and roll over the back of it with a clean roller. Carefully and confidently lift off the block and repeat the pattern, re-inking between each print or every other print.

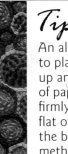

Tip

An alternative method is to place the block ink-side up and carefully lay a sheet of paper over it. Burnish it firmly and evenly with the flat of your hand or with the back of a spoon. This method is only suitable if you are transferring a single large (not a repeat) image.

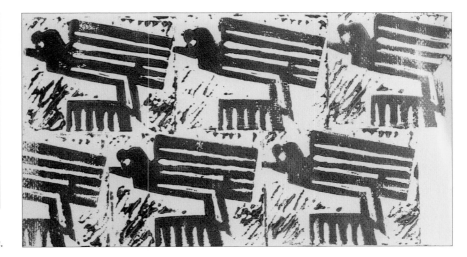

The completed design.

Printing on fabric

1 Tape the washed and ironed fabric to your worksurface as before and mix up your colour on the plate. Transfer the paint to the roller as before and roll it back and forth over the lino block until it has an even coverage of paint.

2 Position the block paint-side down on to the fabric and press firmly and evenly on to the back of the block to transfer the image. I use a clean roller to do this. Lift off the block cleanly to reveal the printed image underneath. Repeat as necessary. When the design is complete, heat-fix the paint as described on page 53.

An Adigraf block printed on to dyed silk fabric to create a border.

Creating texture using lino blocks

A variety of texture marks can be made if you have several different shaped tools and it is worth taking the time to explore the kind of marks that you can make with your collection of tools.

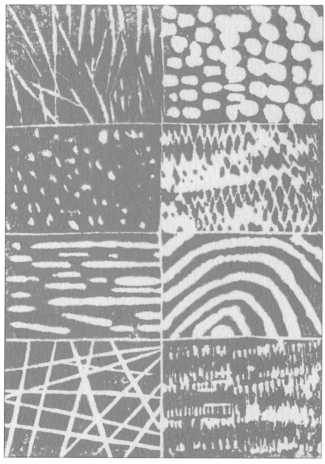

Experiment with different tools to see what marks can be made. These were made into traditional lino.

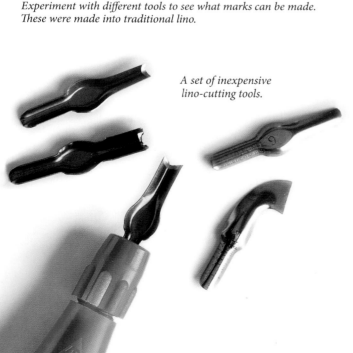

A set of inexpensive lino-cutting tools.

These stipple marks and cross-hatched lines were made into Speedy-carve. They are useful blocks to have as they relate very closely to stitch marks and could be printed to create a background before printing another shape on top.

A variety of textures made with soft-cut lino and a purchased block. Interesting mixtures of colours can be achieved with over-printing and by combining blocks.

Monoprinting

Monoprinting is a method of making a 'one-off' image, with only one print taken from the inked surface, although in practice it is often possible to take two and sometimes three. However, the prints do get successively lighter and more patchy. Although the printing ink has a sticky consistency, it does dry quite quickly, unless mixed with an extender, necessitating a spontaneous approach. Monoprints have a textured, painterly quality which can be very expressive. Because the print is taken quickly, there is usually an energy to the mark made.

The texture achieved by laying dark-coloured fabric over the inked plate and carefully smoothing over the back.

Historically, the process was begun by seventeenth-century artist Giovani Bendetto Castiglioni, who developed it in Rome in 1635. William Blake also used the method, and later it was introduced to the Bauhouse and Modernist movements. Paul Klee, Henri Matisse, George Braque, George Roualt and Marc Chagall all used it, as do many leading contemporary artists around the world.

Ink is applied to a sheet of glass or similar smooth surface, with a hard rubber roller. Thin paper is placed on top of the ink and pressure applied either by hand or by drawing in selected areas on the back with a pencil. When the paper is lifted, only those areas that have had pressure applied to them will be transferred to the paper as a print, although some marks will be transferred as texture, depending on how wet it is or how much ink is on the plate. That, simply put, is the basic method, but as usual there are variations and subtle nuances to the process that are exciting and definitely worth a try. Effects vary from straightforward textural marks to linear imagery and pattern. With a little experimentation, rich and complex surfaces can be achieved.

The printing methods apply to both paper and fabric, and each should be smooth and free from texture and slub. Thin paper and fine fabric work best, but it is always worth experimenting with a variety of surfaces. Use fabric paint for printing on fabric and block-printing ink for paper.

Above: monoprints on paper have been torn up to create a design for a stitched panel.

Left: patchy colours mixed unevenly on the plate give a painterly effect.

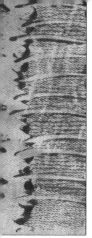

Creating texture

Simply smoothing a piece of paper or fabric with the flat of the hand over an inked plate will give an all-over texture and is ideal as a first print before taking a further print with either a mono technique or with block printing over the top when the ink has dried. Alternatively, make marks in the ink using the end of a paintbrush (as I have done here), a cotton bud, a stick, a knitting needle or any other suitable implement. Interesting effects can also be obtained by drawing into the paint with a piece of rag or screwed-up paper towel, or spraying the surface with water.

MATERIALS

Piece of glass or similar
    smooth surface
Roller
Printing inks, acrylics or
    fabric paint
Palette knife
Paintbrush or other
    mark-making tool
Pencil
Thin paper
Fabric
Paper towel

1 Place the printing ink on to the plate and smooth it out with a roller. If using acrylic paint, add an equal amount of block printing extender and mix with a palette knife. The ink should be evenly distributed over the plate with no lumps or thick areas, and it should sound 'sticky' as you push the roller over the ink. Make marks in the ink with the end of a paintbrush.

2 Place a sheet of thin paper over the ink, taking care not to touch the surface until you are ready to smooth the back of the paper gently with a light pressure using the flat of your hand. This action will give a print with an all-over texture.

3 Lift the paper carefully to reveal the print. If the ink is very thick and heavy, the texture will be more solid but if it is evenly distributed it should give an even, slightly grainy texture.

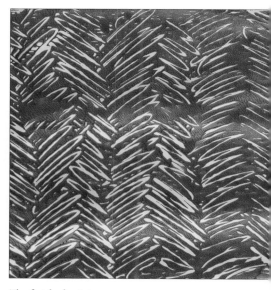

The finished print.

70

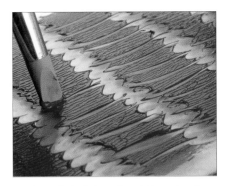

4 Re-roll the ink on the plate and make a different type of mark. I have used a colour shaper to make this pattern.

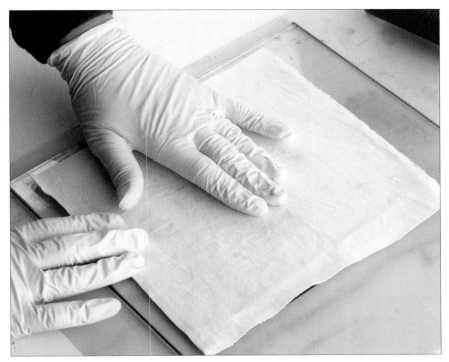

5 Take a print on fabric using the same method as for paper, though you may need to apply a little more pressure on the back of the fabric, using a roller, if needed. The fabric should be fine to medium-weight, and smooth, with all creases ironed out.

6 Carefully lift off the fabric, revealing the print underneath. Leave the fabric to dry thoroughly, then heat-fix as described on page 53.

The finished print. Further prints may be made over fabric already printed with the mono technique. Make sure that the fabric is dry or the colours could run into each other and end up as a muddied image. If you want to preserve part of the print, add a paper resist.

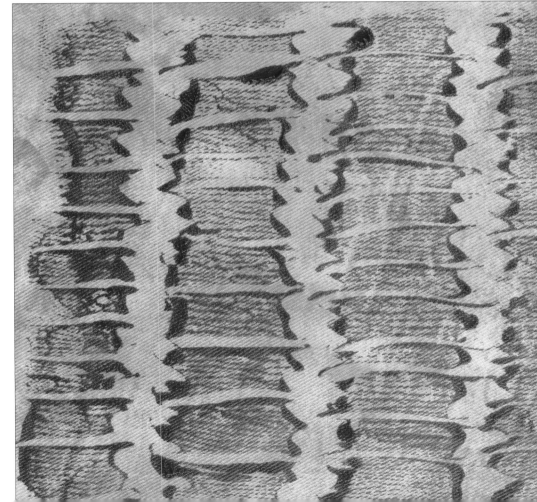

Here, a line was created by drawing into the ink with a cotton bud before taking the print. A colour shaper tool could be used instead.

Creating line

Linear images can easily be created in a monoprint, giving rich black or dark lines, depending on the colour used. Two methods give different effects, one drawing on to the paper or fabric after laying over the ink, and the other drawing into the ink before the paper or fabric is placed.

Method 1

1 Ink up the plate as before and place the paper or fabric over the ink. Draw with a pencil or the end of a paintbrush on the back of the paper firmly, impressing the paper into the inked surface.

2 The lines made will be transferred to the paper or fabric, including any texture that is picked up.

3 Alternatively, take a photocopied design, place it over the inked plate with the image uppermost, and draw over the parts you wish to transfer using a ballpoint pen. Avoid touching the rest of the paper too much.

Method 2

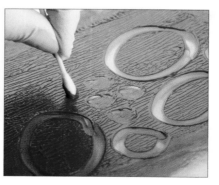 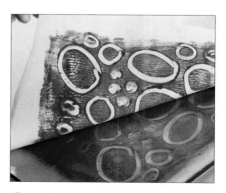

1 Ink up the plate as before and draw into it using a cotton bud.

2 Lay the fabric or paper over the top, press down firmly and lift off.

Mixed colour

More than one colour can be rolled out at a time. Combine two or more colours and part mix them until the ink is evenly distributed, but not completely blended. This will give a multicoloured print. Beware of combining too many colours as you will end up with a mud-coloured print. When prints are dry, further colour can be added by over-printing in a different colour. It is a good idea to begin with the lightest colour and add darker ones on top. If you are using acrylics, washes of colour can be applied over the top of a print once it is dry.

Prints can be made on to dyed fabric, thus achieving a more complex coloured image. Further colour can be added by either over-dying once printing is complete and quite dry, or by painting on washes of silk paint.

This dyed cotton fabric has been printed by laying it on to a sparsely inked two-colour plate. Texture is achieved by stitching into a circle with long crossed stitches. The surrounding area has blocks of couching placed in a tile arrangement using red and yellow thread.

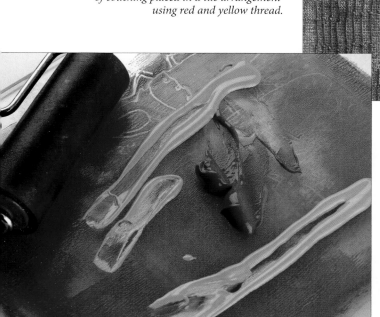

1 Lay out the colours on the glass plate, placing them roughly where you want them to be in the final design.

2 Roll out the paint, being careful not to mix up the colours too much. Print as usual.

Using resists

The process of using paper resists opens up more scope for experimenting. Working with torn or cut paper shapes or paper cuts can produce complex imagery by building up the surface in layers, allowing prints to dry in between the stages. The process works equally well on paper or fabric, but remember that the fabric should be quite flat and works best if it is fine.

1 Ink up the printing plate and lay some thin paper shapes over it. They may have torn edges or be cut with a knife or scissors. I have used two colours on the plate (see page 73). The shapes will prevent the ink from being picked up when the paper or fabric is placed over it.

2 Lay the fabric or paper over the plate and apply pressure (see page 70). Lift the paper gently to reveal the print underneath.

3 It is possible to remove the resists and then take a second print using thin fabric or paper. The fabric or paper will pick up the impression of the resist.

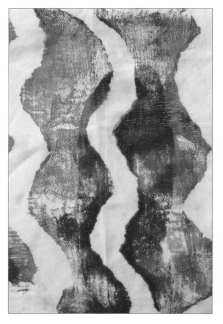

The second print achieved after removing the paper resists.

Lay the inked paper strips over the first print to create another variation on the design.

Creating pattern

This would not be my first choice of method for creating pattern but doily-type patterns can be made successfully using them as a resist. Cut into a piece of thin paper to make a lacy, doily-type paper pattern and lay it carefully over the inked surface. Make sure that it has enough large holes in it, otherwise all that you will have are a few small bits of print, well spaced out, as the paper will act as a resist. Try using actual purchased doilies to create fine detail. You will need to cut away some of the detail to give large enough areas for the ink to be picked up.

1 Carefully place your paper resist on the inked plate. Make sure that all of the paper is in contact with the ink and that the edges are pressed down firmly.

2 Lay your paper or fabric on to the plate, smooth over with a clean roller and lift off to reveal the image underneath.

The completed design.

Using organic resists

This monoprinting technique can be exploited to great effect by adding plant matter in the form of leaves, stems, grasses or flowers to the inked surface. This is not the time to be economical with the ink as enough is needed to thoroughly ink up the organic texture. Place a sheet of paper over the inked texture and smooth the back of it using a hard roller. An imprint of the leaf, or whatever was used, will be transferred to the paper. In addition, if the organic texture is carefully removed, a further print can be taken to lift off the imprint of it from the inked surface. This method is certainly worth a try, as very delicate marks can be achieved. When trying it on fabric, choose a very fine, closely woven cotton or linen, for example handkerchief cotton.

1 Roll out the ink on to the plate as before and lay your selected organic material on the top.

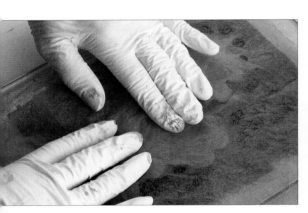

2 Lay a piece of fine fabric over the top and gently but firmly press down on to the leaves.

3 Using a clean roller, gently press the leaves down into the ink, trying not to move them.

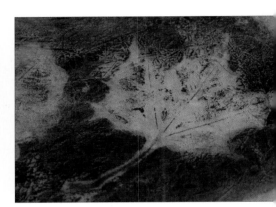

4 Very carefully lift off the fabric, revealing the design.

5 Returning to the plate, carefully remove the leaves to reveal their impressions in the ink underneath.

6 For a subtle design, take a further print to lift off the imprint from the inked surface.

A geranium leaf has been used as a resist on black and yellow paint.

Organic prints from plant material can have a delicate and fragile quality and therefore need a gentle touch. Various leaf prints on to Suede FX and cotton calico have been cut up and reassembled. Fine hand stitching is added to define textures and the textile is mounted on to a painted canvas frame.

Using found objects

An added bonus with print is that many everyday objects that can be found around the home, office or garden can be utilised to create an impression. These items may be recycled or subverted from their usual use, and often cost very little or nothing at all if the item was due to be resigned to the dustbin.

Potatoes

Potatoes make excellent print blocks and have been used at home and in schools with young children for a long time. They can be made very easily with a minimum of cutting, and although they will not last forever, they can be kept in a useable state for quite a few weeks if they are stored in a cool place and wrapped tightly with polythene or plastic food wrap. If you keep them in the fridge, do make sure that the rest of the family know what they are and that they are not consumable!

Other root or hard vegetables can be used in the same way. Try carrots, onions, parsnips or white cabbage. I feel that I need to make the point that I seldom, if ever, use fresh vegetables but prefer to use them if they have gone past their best for edible consumption.

1 Cut a potato in half and dry one surface with a paper towel.

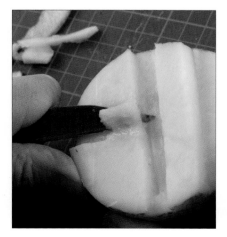

2 Working quickly and spontaneously, cut out the design using a kitchen knife. Use the point of the knife to carve out circles or to create texture.

The finished potato printing block.

3 Apply ink to the raised surfaces using a sponge. Try out the print on a piece of spare paper and trim away the potato to make the surface flatter and more even, if necessary. When you are happy with the result, print on to fabric following the method on pages 52–53.

A further print is added, offsetting the motif to make a more complex image.

Right: seeding enhances a potato-printed cotton fabric, adding a rich texture.

Above: the red patterning here was first potato-printed in white on the dark background fabric and then over-printed in bright red.

Washers

Washers made from metal, cloth, rubber or plastic can all be transformed into printing devices. Individually, they are best stuck to the end of a short length of wooden dowel, making it easier to make a print, or several may be combined and stuck to stiff card or a piece of wood. I prefer to work with either cloth or rubber as these materials hold the ink or paint better.

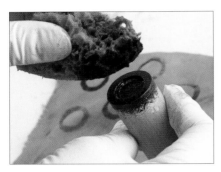

1 Apply ink to the washer-end of the wooden block using a small piece of sponge.

2 Stamp the image repeatedly over the fabric or paper, re-inking the washer to strengthen the image at regular intervals.

3 Repeat the process with a different-coloured ink, if required.

Cardboard

Card held on its edge will print successfully. If the edge is cut into, the print will make broken lines or stippled lines. These can be curved if the card is carefully bent. Using corrugated card gives a wavy line, and it can be rolled up to make a spiral. Stick layers together to get broader marks or change the direction of the card.

Make a block by gluing together several layers of corrugated card. Apply ink to the edge of the block and stamp a pattern over the surface of the paper or fabric. Make a second block by rolling up another piece of card and use a different colour to stamp a complementary design over the first.

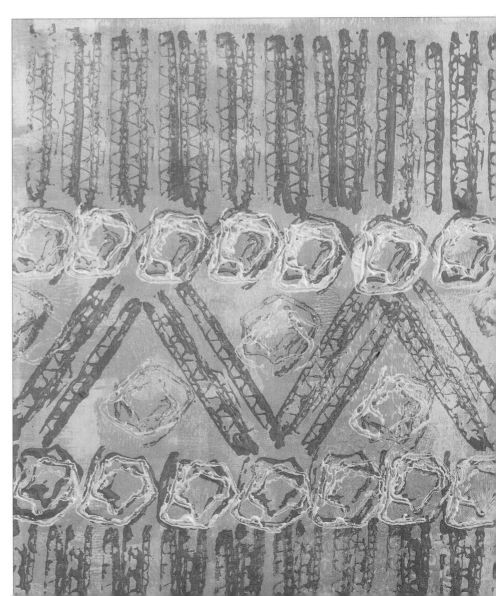

This folded square box is printed with a washer block on to dyed silk fabric bonded to cotton. The decoration is on the outside of the shape and the inside is plain. The corners are decorated with machine-made florets. These are made by stitching across a hole cut into a piece of fabric that is stretched into a frame. The stitching is cut out and used as decoration.

This box is folded with the printed surface inside. The cotton fabric is printed with a piece of thick corrugated card and has machine stitching added in a complementary colour. The edges of the pointed rim are decorated with tiny beads.

Sponge printing

Sponges, whether natural or man-made, are very easy to print with and inexpensive too. Various types can be used, from washing-up sponges and make-up sponges, to those designed for car cleaning, upholstering furniture or packaging. Foam or sponge is easy to cut with scissors or a scalpel and different types will give a variety of textures, some with large, open holes and others with a close-grained texture.

Mark the design on the sponge surface with a felt-tip pen and cut away the areas not wanted. When printing with a sponge block, care is needed when making the print, particularly when it is freshly charged with ink or paint. Because the sponge is flexible and holds a fair amount of paint, a very light touch is required – not much pressure is needed to make the print.

1 Cut the sponge to the desired size using a scalpel.

2 Draw on the design using a marker pen or felt-tip pen (neither pencil nor ballpoint pen are suitable).

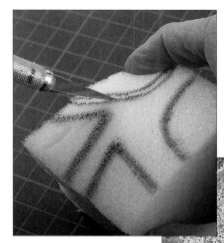

3 Cut down into the sponge along the edges of the design using either a scalpel or a pair of small, sharp scissors.

4 Work with sharp, pointed scissors to snip away the surplus sponge to a depth of about 3–4mm (¼in).

The finished sponge block.

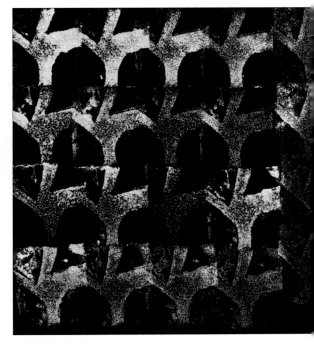

5 Put some printing ink on to a palette and dip the sponge into it. Dab it lightly a few times to obtain an even coating of ink (use fabric paint if you are printing on to fabric). Apply the sponge firmly and rock it gently back and forth to make an impression. The more downward pressure you exert, the more of the background will be transferred. Because the sponge will hold a lot of ink, several prints can be made before needing to re-charge it.

The finished pattern.

Two prints using the same sponge. On the left I have drawn into the print with dots and added some yellow paint. On the right, I have first printed with yellow and then printed again using green. The prints show the characteristic texture that it is possible to achieve using a sponge block.

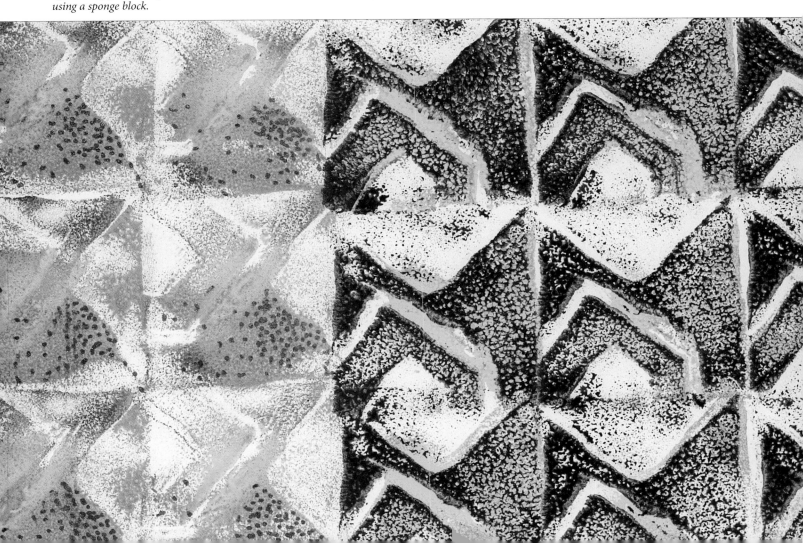

Collagraph printing

A collagraph print is one made from a block that is constructed from low-level collaged material. This type of printing has enjoyed a popularity boost in recent times and the process has become very refined. Ideally, printing is done with a press, but good results can be achieved without using one, although it may be necessary to use smaller blocks rather than larger ones. Collagraph blocks may be organised in the form of 'jigsaw' blocks. That is, separate blocks that may have different textures and shapes but which fit together to make a whole. Jigsaw blocks can be a method of achieving a larger print.

The materials used for the block may be paper, glue, string, textured paper found in packaging, doilies, crumpled paper, cloth, netting, flat leaves, grass or any other material that has very little dimension to it. Anaglypta wallpaper is very effective, as is cutting away the top layer of the base card. This can be done by scoring the card with a scalpel to make a shape, then lifting off the layer of card, leaving a section that is now lower than the rest of the surface. This section will not print when the block is inked up.

Care needs to be taken to ensure that if different types of materials are used to create a block, the level remains constant. If there is variation in levels, some of the textures will print and some will not.

Several collagraph blocks were used to print the cotton fabric for this circular bag. The fabric was embellished with machine zigzag spirals and free running stitch. A contrast band around the top edge carries the twisted cord to close. The bag is lined with dyed silk.

1 Cut a piece of thick card to the required size and coat it with PVA glue using an old, stiff paintbrush.

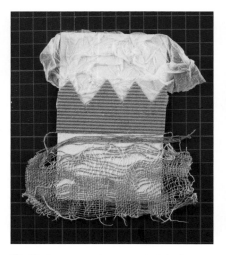

2 Stick on your chosen materials. I have used crumpled tissue paper for the top layer, then corrugated card cut with a zigzag edge, and finally a piece of scrim, torn to give it a distressed look. Press down all the materials firmly and make sure they are all at a similar height, otherwise you will obtain an irregular print.

3 Trim off the surplus material and leave to dry. You should now seal the surface with quick-drying button polish or water-resistant varnish and leave for 24 hours to dry thoroughly.

4 To print on to fabric, tape the fabric down to your worksurface (see page 52) and roll out a single colour of ink on to your plate. Here I have scraped away a section of the first colour and spooned in a second colour to add variety.

5 Roll the two colours carefully to avoid mixing them together. The idea is to leave a distinct strip of the second colour through the centre of the first.

6 Ink up the block as described on page 64 and lay it face down on the fabric. Apply pressure to the back of the block as before, using a clean roller. Lift off the block and repeat.

Tip

Alternatively, the block can be inked up using a sponge (see page 50). A more successful print may be taken if the paper is placed over the block and burnished with either the fingers, a spoon or a baren. Pressure is applied by rubbing the back of the paper.

The completed print.

Bubblewrap

Bubblewrap and plastic food wrap will give circles, curly textures or a scrumpled print. Stick them to card or wood for a regular effect or screw up into a ball and print to get texture. This technique is best suited to fairly sturdy materials such as faux suede (e.g. Suede FX).

1 Begin by rolling out the ink or fabric paint on a glass printing plate. Pick up the colour using a roller and transfer it to the bubblewrap block.

2 Lay the block face down on to paper or fabric and apply pressure evenly with a clean roller. Lift off the block.

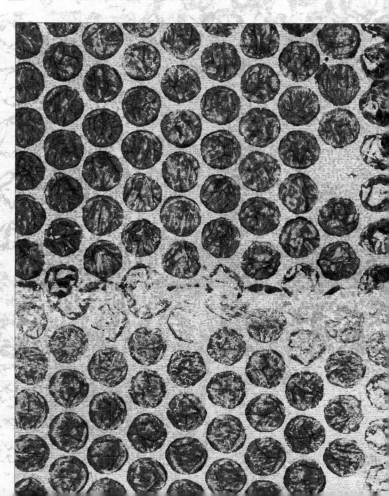

3 Repeat the design over the fabric to create an interesting background for stitch.

String

For a linear print, stick string to a piece of stout card or wood. Either attach double-sided tape to the card or wood and then stick the string to it, or soak the string in PVA glue and then attach it to the support and leave to dry. The first method is easier but the second is more durable.

Buttons

Thermoplastic foam such as Softsculpt can be used to make printing blocks. When heated, hard items can be impressed into it, in this case buttons. The foam imprint is then fixed to strong card.

This string print has split stitch and coral stitch worked on top. Care has to be taken not to cover the print completely.

A block of mouldable thermoplastic foam (Softsculpt) has been impressed with buttons and the design printed on to fabric. It is embellished with a pleasing combination of straight stitch and buttonhole rings.

Other materials

Any natural material such as wood or cork can be used to create texture; also nails, screws, sticks or anything hard that can be pressed into thermoplastic memory foam to create a print block. Tile spacers or any other plastic component stuck to card or wood can also be used to make interesting designs. Balsa wood used for model making is soft enough to indent with a ballpoint pen. It is very easy to make an impression and it prints beautifully. The wood is available in sheets or blocks.

Stitching can be stuck to a piece of thin wood or thick card and used to print with. The thread used for the stitching should be quite thick or the impression will not show up very well. Use a loosely woven fabric so that you can draw the thread through it easily. You will find that the stitched surface flattens as printing progresses.

Above: a print taken from a balsa-wood block, printed with white paint on to dark fabric, creating a rather ghostly image.

Right: a card tube is wound around with string and rolled into paint. It is then rolled over the surface of the fabric to create a linear texture. A further texture block is over-printed with a different colour.

Left: these tiny gift boxes have been painted and printed using washers, corrugated card and foam circles. Machine-stitched florets, beads and printed motifs are added to decorate the boxes further.

Textured rollers

Elastic bands, string or strips of torn cloth can be wrapped around a stout
card roll and used like a rolling pin. Small decorating rollers designed for
painting behind radiators can be cut into to make patterns or texture marks
before rolling over a surface.

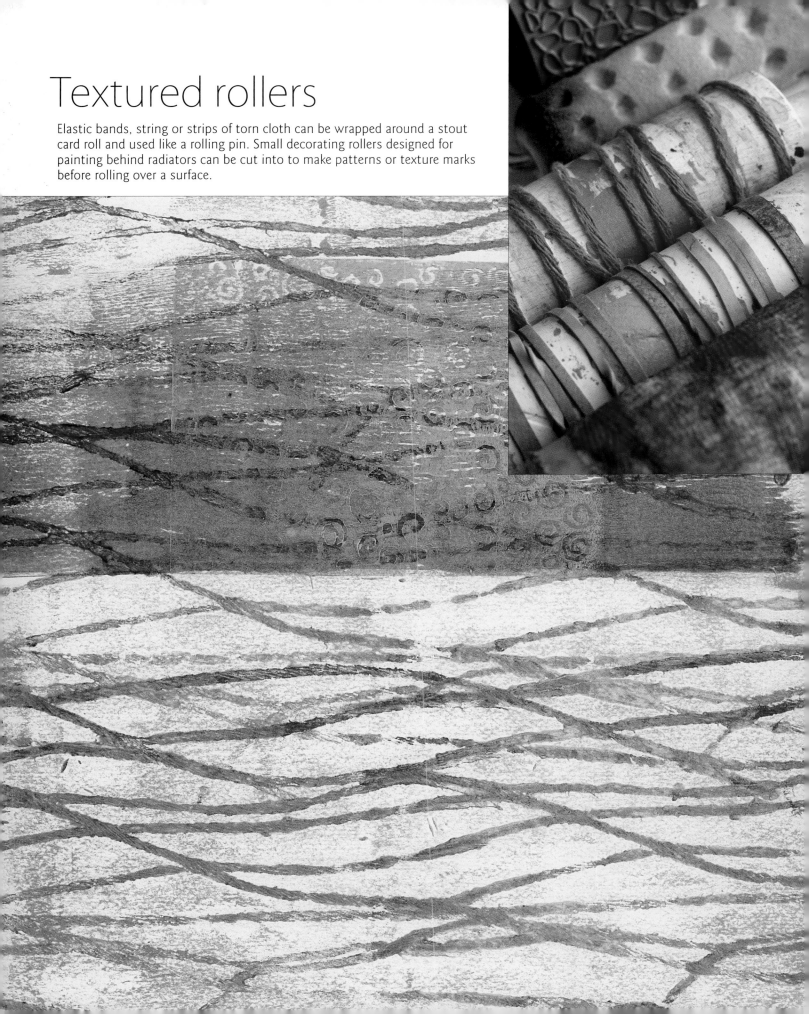

STITCHING

Adding stitch to an otherwise flat surface can transform a piece of cloth into an exciting and vibrant textile to be enjoyed just as it is or to put to any number of uses, decorative or practical. I enjoy print for its own sake as well as for the creative potential that it presents. Print can be appealing and satisfying in its own right and has a long history of being so. The difficulty with combining print with stitch is in deciding how and what type of stitching to use. Keep in mind the balance between the stitching and the print; the stitching should enhance the print rather than overwhelm it. The two aspects should be fully integrated, the two techniques working together, neither one or the other dominating; a tricky balance to achieve.

Often the print will suggest a mark or texture that will help to select an appropriate method of stitching, whether by hand or machine. Hand stitching usually gives a more raised surface while machine stitching will give a flatter effect. The two methods worked in tandem can produce variety and interest.

The purpose of the fabric you are printing on should also be taken into account. What will the fabric be used for and how much wear will it get? Will the fabric need to be laundered? Perhaps it is intended to be purely decorative, in which case some of the practical issues can be put aside and the imagination allowed to run riot.

Practice in using a stitch can build up a valuable library of experience, and the working of samples can throw up the potential benefits or problems of a particular technique. It is worth spending time experimenting with techniques, trying them on a variety of fabrics with different threads and on different kinds of print. Some fabrics, although good for stitch, may not take the print well. Usually firm weaves work best but this will rule out thicker threads as they cannot be pulled through the fabric. The print itself will stiffen the fabric to an extent, but it will soften up as stitching progresses. The stiffness can be an advantage on finer fabrics, giving some body to them and often negating the need for using a frame.

If you want the effect of thick threads, other techniques need to be employed. They can be couched on to the surface with a fine thread or by machine, or whipped around stitches already made. They can be woven in and out of surface stitching or worked separately and applied in the form of a slip.

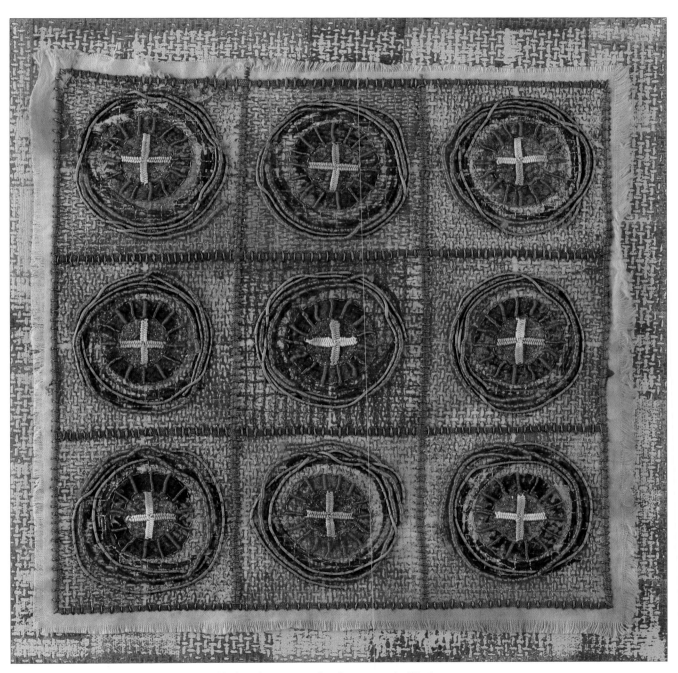

Dyed fabric has been printed with a texture block and over-printed with various relief blocks. A string block creates a linear mark that works well with the couched line. The centres of the circles have a needlewoven cross, surrounded by whipped straight stitches. The panel is mounted on to a purchased canvas frame that is printed with the same texture block as that used for the textile.

Starting to stitch

Whether or not you place your work in a frame is a personal choice, as some people like to hold the fabric in the hand. If you are using a frame, make sure that as you move it around it does not crush or distort the stitching already done. It is also not a good idea to leave the fabric in the frame for too long when not stitching, as it will mark the fabric and the stitching. Some techniques require framing, especially machine methods, for example free machining, cable and whip stitch (see page 124).

Hand stitching

1 Heat-fix your printed fabric (see page 53) and lay it on to a piece of backing fabric. This should not be too heavy or densely woven (calico is ideal). Pin or tack the two together if you wish.

2 Place the fabric in an embroidery hoop and tighten so that it is taut and even. Make sure you choose a hoop that is an appropriate size for your chosen design. If possible, the design should sit comfortably in the middle of the hoop, so there is no need to reposition the hoop as you work.

3 Now start to stitch! Add suitable stitching worked in a colour that complements or matches the printed design. Start with a simple stitch and add other, more decorative stitches worked in different threads until you achieve the desired effect.

The thickness of the threads and the type of needle you can use are dictated by the density of the fabric – the more closely woven the fabric, the thinner the threads and the finer the needle you can work with.

This sample shows a further devlopment of the stitched surface. Cross stitches in pink divide the blue squares and fly stitches are worked on to the blue, adding texture without changing the colour.

Machine stitching

There are many excellent books on machine embroidery so I will concentrate on the aspects of the machine that I use to create my surfaces. Further details about working specific stitches are given on pages 116–125.

The very nature of machine embroidery is to create a stitched surface on the fabric with the thread. This means that the surface will become completely covered with thread. If this is done over a printed surface, it rather takes away the need for print as none of it will be seen, unless print is the method of transferring the design.

So the machine needs to be used in a rather different way to embellish and complement the print rather than hide it.

1 Set up the sewing machine for free running by lowering the feed dogs and putting on the darning foot. Slacken the top tension to 3 on the dial.

2 Secure the fabric in a hoop so that the back of the fabric is flush with the edge of the hoop and place it on the sewing plate with the front uppermost. Before starting to stitch, pull up the bobbin thread. When you have done a few stitches, the thread ends can be cut off so that they are not distracting and do not get tangled while you are stitching.

Left: a detail of the monoprinted casket shown opposite. The printed fabric has been stitched by machine using free running stitch, allowing the print to show through.

Above: the same casket with the door closed.

This casket has been developed from a geometric shape, a hexagon. I worked out the shape with its details in paper and card first (shown below). This enabled me to see what separate shapes were needed to build the casket and what size they needed to be. I have covered the mock-up with a charcoal drawing that I made of a collection of bottles and boxes. The design wraps around the shape in a more organic manner with detail flowing from one panel to the next.

The textile casket (right) was made in the same way. I drew on to dyed calico with heat-fixable charcoal in black, grey and white. The fabric was decorated with free machine stitching to embellish the drawing. I used the resulting cloth to cover the box form.

Stitch gallery

There are many excellent books available on stitches and on machine embroidery so I am just including a few of my favourites which I have found over time to be useful and that give me the effects I am looking for. I tend not to use stitches that have a complicated structure but favour instead the ones that derive from a straight stitch.

I have divided the stitches into stitch families, and included a sampler of ideas followed by some stitched samples. Not all the ideas are illustrated with a stitched example, but the drawings should give a good idea of how the stitches could look. Some of the samples include a combination of stitches in response to the colour and marks within the print. The joy of stitching for me is in selecting thread with the right texture and colour to complement the print fully and not having to struggle with technique.

Left: a lino block has been printed in white on black fabric. Parts of the design are machine stitched with a variegated thread and seeding by hand is used to texture the remaining areas.

Right: the same lino block is used to print in black on white fabric that is worked by machine within the black areas of the print. Using a circular stitching motion with black thread, a fine texture is achieved. Cross-hatched texture is made on to the remaining areas using a coloured, variegated thread.

Hand stitches

Stitches for line

The straight stitch family of stitches includes seeding, satin, cross-hatching, running stitch and back stitch. These are my favourite stitches, as they are so versatile. They can be any length, can be placed in any direction, and are as effective worked with thick threads as with fine, and all grades in between. They are mark-making stitches, ideal to use for drawing, and can be endlessly varied for more painterly effects.

There are many stitches that can be worked in a line and used as edgings or for outlining. Here are a few that are effective but it is worth remembering that they can all be used in other ways too.

When choosing a stitch, consider the quality or type of line that you want. A line can be crisp and continuous, broken, fine or wide, a double line, fuzzy, woolly, fibrous, frilly or knobbly. Consider too, the quality of thread you could use to match that of the line. Threads may be smooth or rough, shiny or matt, thick or thin. They are made from cotton, silk, linen or rayon and can be slubby or have a sheen.

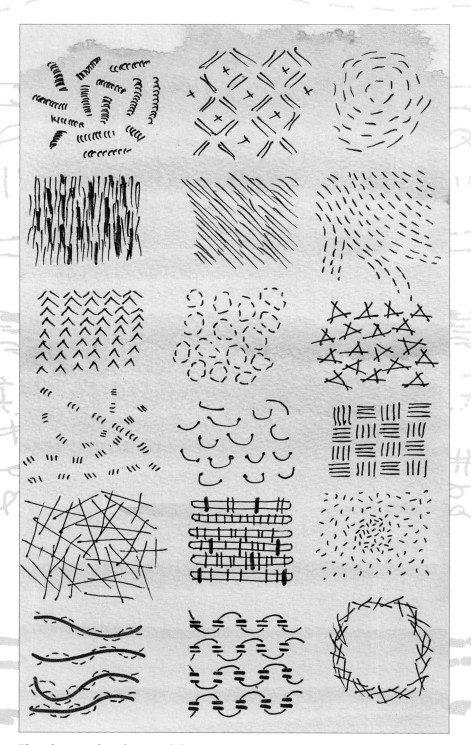

These diagrams show the many different textures and marks that can be achieved using straight stitches. Most can be adapted to create a line.

Couching

Running

Open chain

Zigzag chain

Satin

Back stitch

Threaded running

Couching

Twisted chain

Stem

Split

Chain and open chain

Twisted and zigzag chain

Herringbone

Cretan

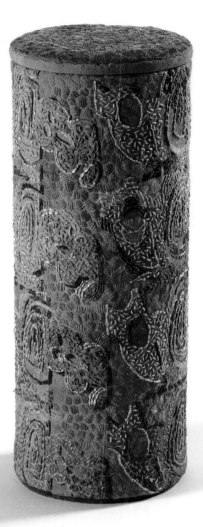

Dyed cotton fabric was first printed with a texture block and over-printed with a relief block. A second print in a different colour gives a dark ghosting around the shape. The resulting fabric is decorated with hand stitching to create a surface texture. The stitches used are seeding, couching and blocks of satin stitch in the background. The finished textile is stretched over a strong card tube to make a vessel, and lined with felt. The lid is printed with a texture block and hand stitched with blocks of satin stitch.

The detail (left) shows the contrast between the seeding and blocks of satin stitch.

Images on facing page

Top left: a dyed fabric was printed with a relief block, which is edged with back stitch. The surrounding area is textured with free running by machine. The flowers have satin stitch at their centres.

Top right: straight stitch is used to decorate this potato print. Thick thread is couched down with tiny straight stitches and a broad braid is held with longer straight stitches. A mixture of rayon and cotton threads are used to provide contrast of surface.

Bottom left: a block of mouldable thermoplastic foam (Softsculpt) has been impressed with buttons to create a block. The print is defined using straight stitches around the circles and running stitch as a contrast. The spaces between the circles are filled with French knots for texture.

Bottom right: a dyed cotton fabric had paint dragged across it and was then printed with a variety of circular blocks of different sizes. The print is embellished with straight stitches of differing sizes and fly stitches. Free running stitch by machine is worked into the surrounding spaces.

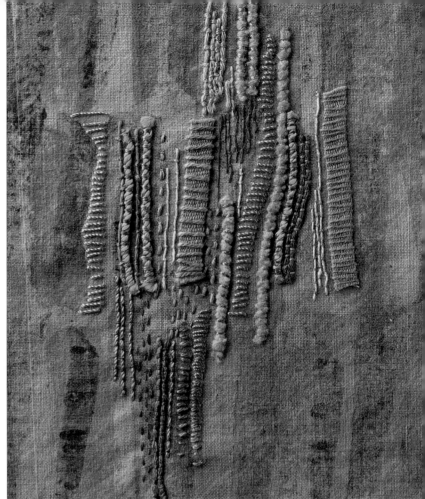
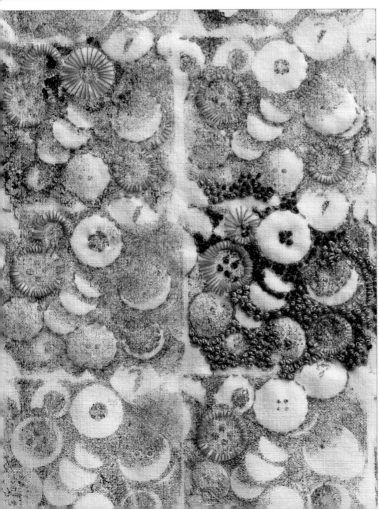
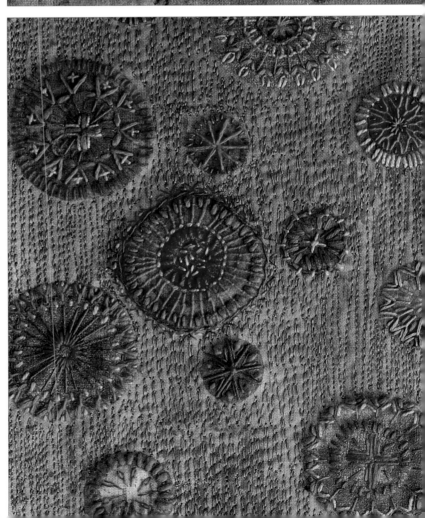

Buttonhole stitch

Buttonhole stitch is useful as an edging, along with its close associate, blanket stitch. Both can also be worked as fillings, with the 'prongs' of the stitch varied in length and placing. Parts of the shape of the stitch can be whipped to add further dimension, and patterns may be made into which other stitches can be placed. Lines of buttonhole stitch can be placed back to back, and in curves. Interesting raised effects can be achieved with detached buttonhole stitch, creating flaps of stitching, or by working on to straight stitches to create raised lines.

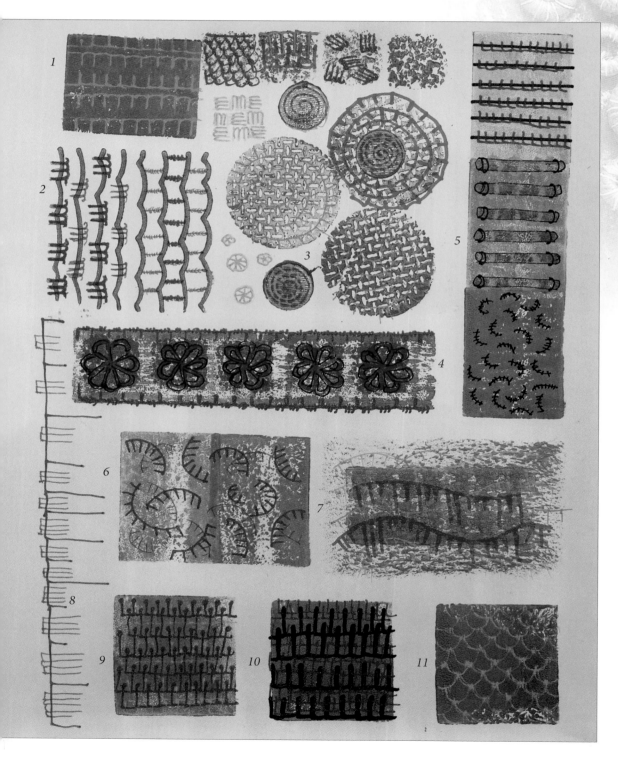

1 Back-to-back
2 Couching bars
3 Spirals
4 Buttonhole wheels
5 Couched buttonhole stitch
6 Broken textural stitching
7 Overlapping
8 Line
9 Knotted
10 Interlocking
11 Detached

Buttonhole stitch can be used in many different ways, as seen in this diagram.

A block of mouldable thermoplastic foam (Softsculpt) was impressed with buttons to create a block. The resulting print was embellished with buttonhole stitch worked in circles. Buttonhole rings have been made separately and applied over the stitching.

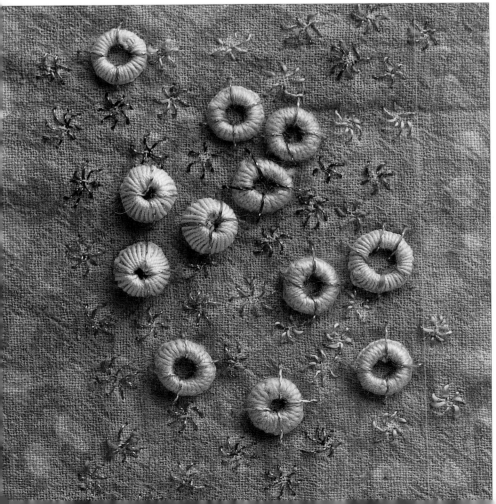

A texture print was made on to green fabric and buttonhole rings sewn on to the circular marks with added straight stitches arranged in tiny circles. Some of the buttonhole rings were made over a wooden or plastic former.

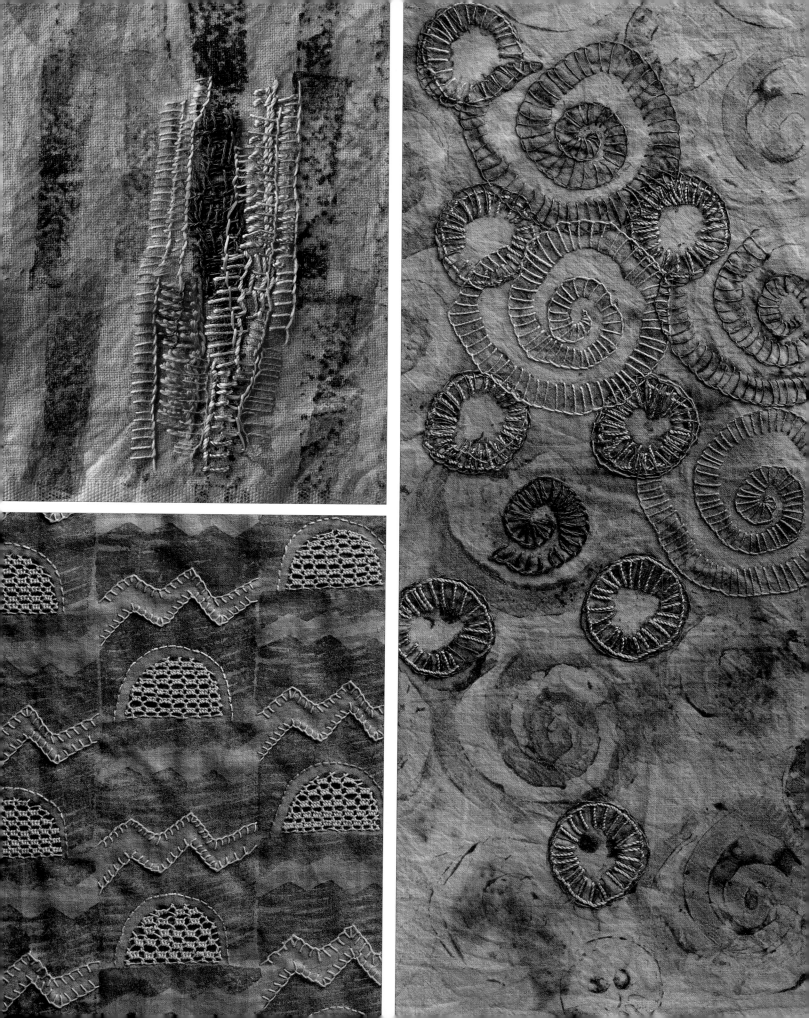

Images on facing page

Top left: buttonhole stitch and seeding are worked on to this potato print. The buttonhole is overlapped and built up to create texture.

Bottom left: fabric was printed with a textured roller before a further print was made over the top. Using cotton perle thread, a buttonhole edging creates bands that contrast with the domed shapes. These were filled with Brussels stitch – a needlelace stitch that is a variation of buttonhole stitch.

Right: a purchased foam block in the shape of a spiral and a block made from impressed foam were used here to create an all-over pattern which is decorated with buttonhole stitch.

Buttonhole rings were worked separately, some over a wooden mould, and stitched on to a printed surface to give a strong textural effect.

Couching

Another stitched method that has an illustrious history, being the main stitch used in Opus Anglicanum and the Bayeux Tapestry during the early to late Middle Ages, couching is the basis of all laid work. It is an ideal method for outlining an edge or for use as a filling, with several variations to choose from. It is a good choice when thick threads are to be laid on the surface of the fabric and held down with a finer one. Parts of the line made can be whipped for a raised effect, or a core thread could be held with a close satin stitch to create a smooth, raised line.

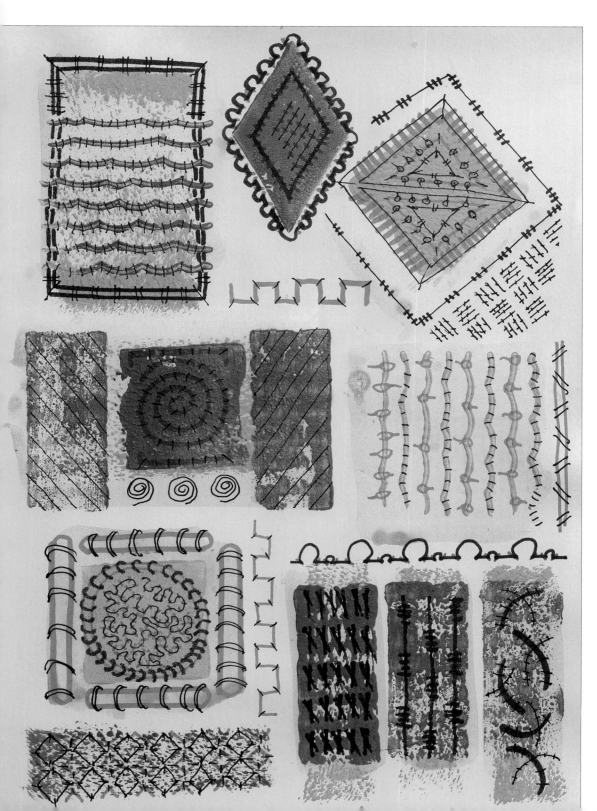

Suggested arrangements for couching.

Images on facing page

Top left: a soft woollen fabric has been roller printed for texture and then enhanced with couched lines and running stitch.

Top right: the print is embellished with lines of couching using a cotton thread. The direction of stitching is varied in response to the print.

Bottom left: marbled fabric is over-printed with a monoprint, creating circles. These are defined with couching, and cretan stitch is worked in between.

Bottom right: a monoprint has couched lines of soft, untwisted silk thread, laid in a grid into which seeding is worked. The colour lightens and brightens towards the centre.

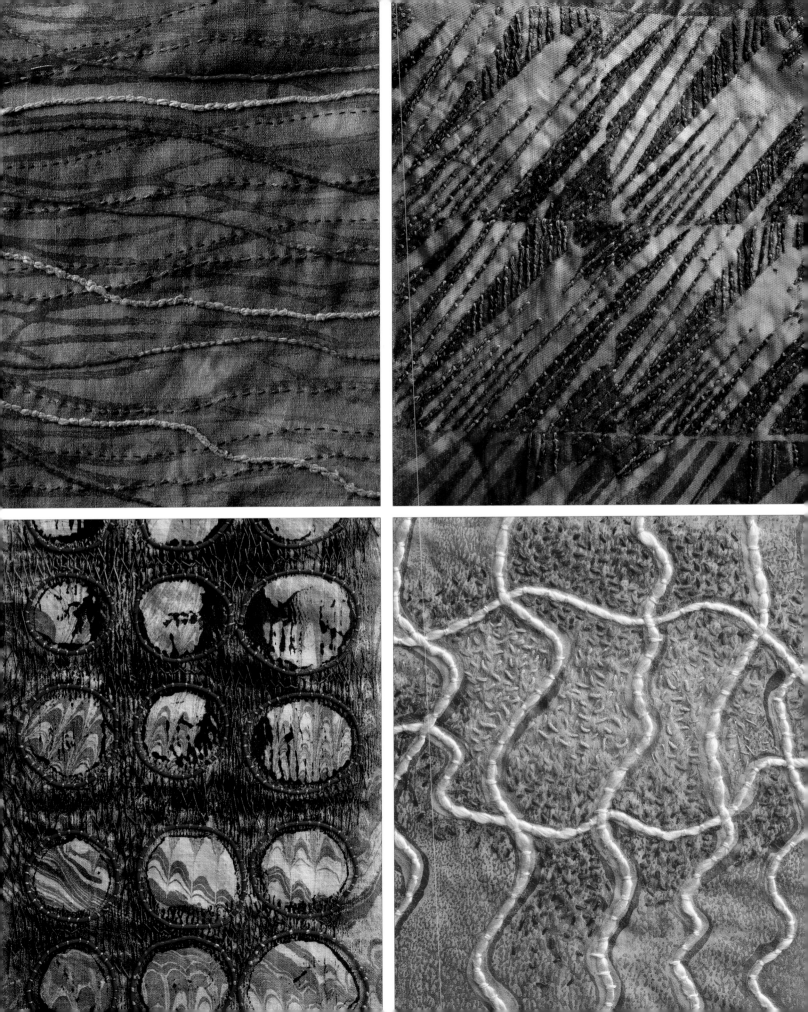

Chain stitch

This is a stitch that is found on textiles all over the world. It has many variations, and can be used as a line stitch or as a filling. Interesting raised effects can be achieved with detached chain, creating flaps of stitching, and when used singly it is possible to create any number of patterns depending on how the stitch is formed. The heads can be tiny with long tails or reversed with the heads large and wide with short tails, ideal for placing into a grid of squares. Other variations may be whipped or twisted. Many patterns can be made just by changing the placement and proportions of the stitches. To create texture, the stitches may be positioned in grids, circles or lines, or placed randomly.

Images on facing page

Top: detached chain stitch is arranged within the printed squares with tails meeting in the centres. Various threads are used including rayon, silk and cotton perle.

Bottom left: a collagraph print is embellished with detached chain arranged in a grid pattern. The blue tails meet at the corners of the squares and the heads in the centres. The black and grey stitches are arranged around the squares with the heads meeting at the intersections. Complementary colours of blue and orange are used with the single circle of orange placed into a square and blended into the background with orange stitches.

Bottom right: various forms of chain stitch are used for this potato-print sample. Open chain is placed over lines of regular chain to build up the surface texture. Zigzag chain is used in the same way. Differing types and thickness of thread are combined to give variety.

The diagram shows the many variations of detached chain stitch.

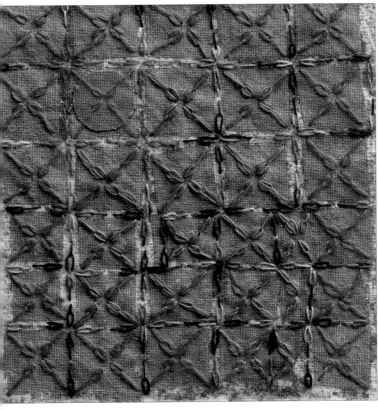

Fly stitch

This stitch is sometimes called 'Y' stitch as it makes the shape of a 'Y'. Fly stitches can be placed together to make patterns, work well in grids and are useful, too, for creating a soft-edged line by extending the centre part and narrowing the 'V'.

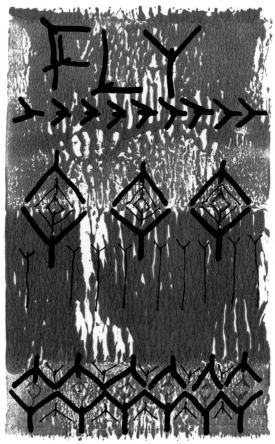

Suggested arrangements for the use of fly stitch.

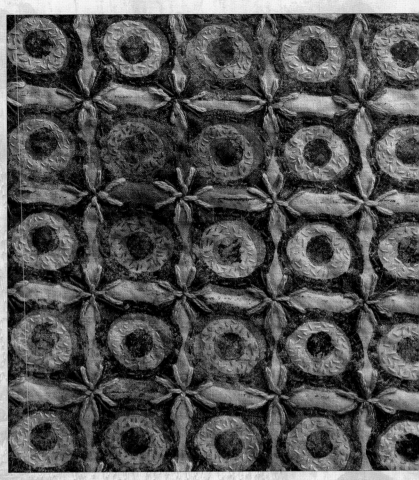

Fly stitch is arranged around the corners of the collagraph print. The central area is stitched in a contrasting colour and blends outwards while the turquoise blends into the pink/red area, thus meshing the two contrasting colours together and softening the division between them.

An eraser block print on dyed cotton fabric is embellished with seeding in the circles and fly stitches at the intersections. A running stitch in red surrounds the circles.

Fly stitch is used in these circles together with chain and straight stitches.

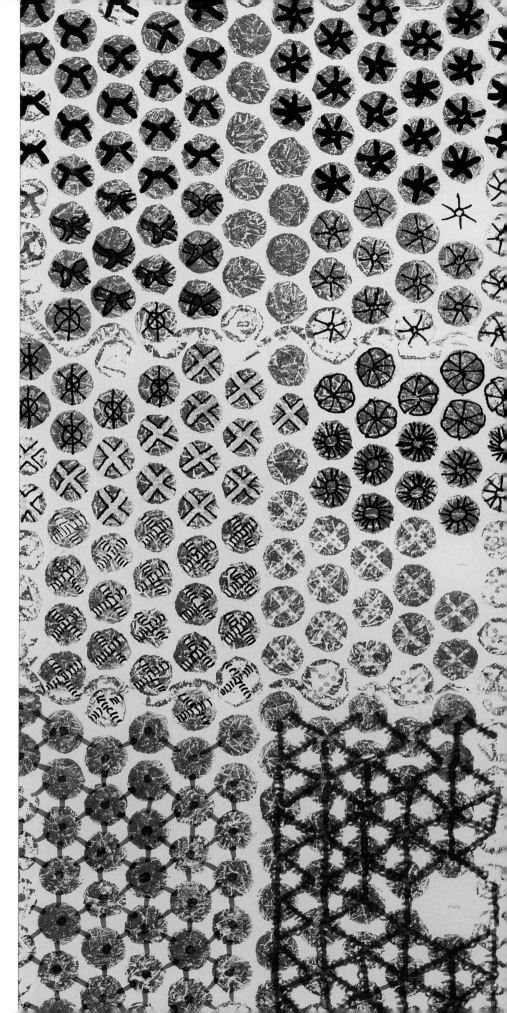

Sorbello stitch

Here is a knotted stitch that may be worked regularly in rows or, more excitingly, randomly, varying the shape. When worked in a regular method, it makes a square shape, with four corners and the knot in the centre. It can be varied by making the 'legs' different lengths so that it looks spidery, or given a more solid knot when a thick thread is used. Lumps and bumps can be made by piling up the stitches on top of one another.

The drawing shows some ideas for embellishing circles, including sorbello, which may be whipped or layered up. Circles lend themselves to buttonhole stitch and to being linked with straight stitches. These may also be whipped for further texture or have beads added.

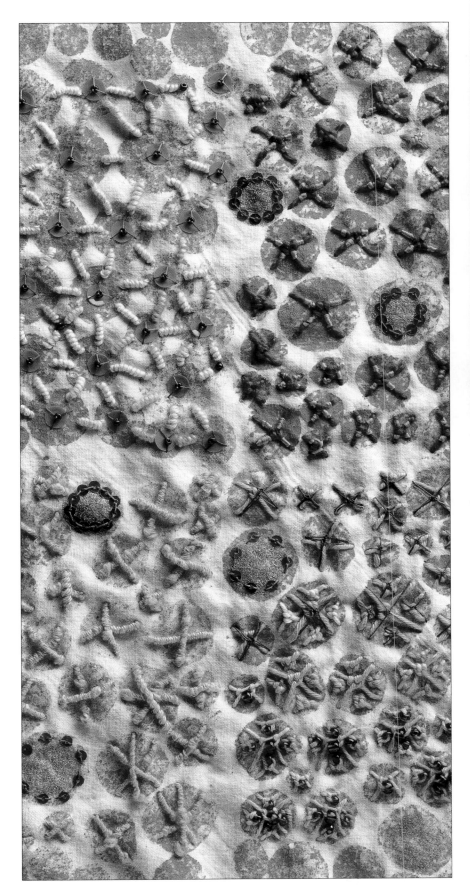

Above: sorbello has been worked on to a block print, with several stitches piled one on top of another. These are laced with a thread that runs underneath each stitch, creating a grid that slightly puckers the fabric, producing a ruched effect.

Left: this sample shows sorbello, sorbello with added beads, whipped straight stitch and whipped cross stitch.

Composite stitches

These are worked in two stages. A foundation layer of stitches is laid down first and the second stage is worked on to these. Many effects can be achieved using combinations of stitch structures, varying the type, thickness and colour of thread.

The sample shows what the stitches look like and includes raised chain band, raised stem, whipped running, whipped straight, interlaced herringbone, whipped chain and wave stitch.

A diagram of the composite stitches shown in the sample.

Right: a variety of composite stitches is shown. Working clockwise from top left these are: raised chain band, threaded running, whipped zigzag chain, threaded running, raised chain band in a circle with interlaced cross stitch in the centre, raised stem band, sheaf stitch in a circle with whipped straight stitch in the centre, interlaced herringbone along the bottom, raised stem band in a circle with wave stitch in centre, whipped back stitch with wave in centre.

Machine stitches

There are fewer individual stitches when it comes to working by machine, but a great variety of surface textures can be achieved when responding to the marks made by print. There are also foot attachments that may help to introduce further textures such as a cording foot or a tailor's tacking foot to create a tufted effect, or an eyelet foot. Adding and subtracting fabric can make a difference too, through either layering or cutting away.

A texture print is decorated with machine zigzag using a variegated thread. Straight stitches, worked by hand in complementary orange, are placed in between the lines of machining.

The same print but a different colour has been stitched by machine using a free running stitch to edge the lines of the print. Machine tufting is added to part of the sample.

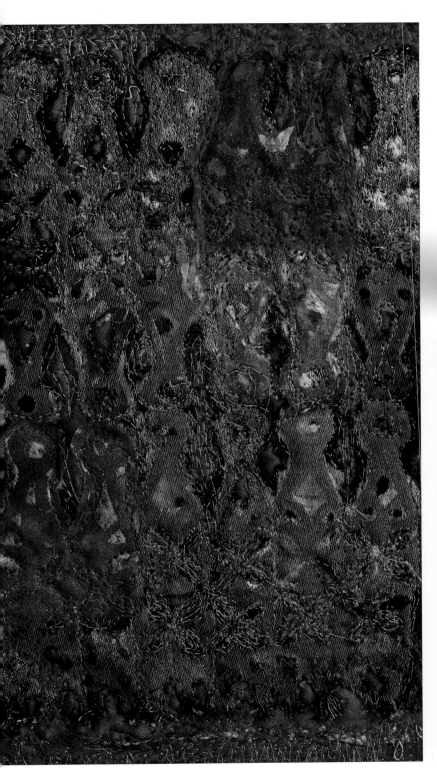

This print is made with an eraser block and is used to create a textile to add to the front of a key box. I wanted to achieve the effect of an old, worn textile. To achieve this, a layer of printed fabric was placed over the red fabric and the two layers stitched together by machine using free running. Areas of the top fabric have been cut away and more print added. Edges have been allowed to fray and the detail is fragmented.

Top: the key box.
Above: detail showing texture.

Free running stitch

This is an extremely useful stitch technique and one that I use most of the time. It is possible to make a very dense area of stitching or to navigate around edges of shapes, or to meander around a surface in order to texture it and adjust the colour of the background.

I like to use the needle as a drawing tool and make marks as if I were using a pen, pencil or a brush. Working with the feed dogs down or covered, and a darning foot to replace the normal sewing foot, allow you to make marks with the stitching to create an endless number of effects, just as you would with drawing tools. Very delicate marks can be achieved or bold, definite ones when cable stitch (see page 124) is employed.

Straight lines spaced at about 3mm (⅛in) are¼ a good method of filling a space or shape without obliterating the print, and when they are made with free running stitch, they have a more 'relaxed' look to them. If they are made with the machine set for ordinary sewing, that is, with the feed dogs up and the normal sewing foot on, they can be very stiff and clinical and it is not possible to go round corners easily as the work has to be constantly turned around. Free running stitch gives flexibility.

Tip
Take care when using the machine for free running and keep fingers well away from the needle area. Turn the machine off when attending to maintenance and changing needles.

Line

Echoed outlines

Filling

Directional line

Texture

Spots

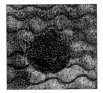

Curved line

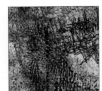

Cross hatching

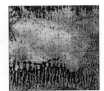

Texture

Couching

Outline shapes

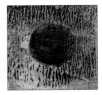

Spiral

Facing page: this sample shows examples of free running stitch by machine. The key above provides details of the techniques used.

Left: free running is applied to a monoprint that has been placed on to wadding thus creating a lightly quilted effect.

Far left: a print was made on to dissolvable plastic and machine stitch added. Individual motifs were linked using a contrast thread colour. When the plastic was dissolved away, an open, lacy fabric was left behind.

Left: a leaf print on to a dyed silk and cotton mix fabric is edged with free machining. The fabric is backed with wadding to give a quilted look. This technique is best done in a frame.

Below: various monoprints on cotton fabric were combined using lines of free running stitch. The image of a vessel was left free of stitching so that it stands out.

Zigzag stitch

Working with free zigzag stitching gives an opportunity to blend colour, but it does need space to develop its qualities. It is ideal for texturing a background between prints or to add texture to a relatively simple and open print. Small, complicated shapes are best embroidered with a free running stitch closely worked. When the fabric is moved from side to side, a lot of thread can be laid on to the surface and it is a good way of making thicker lines. It is good to use on textured prints as it does not have to be kept within a shape. Free zigzag comes into its own when making machine cords. Working backwards and forwards, it is possible to cover a core thread easily and to blend the colours as one is laid over the previous layer of stitching.

Side-to-side zigzag

Side-to-side zigzag overlapping colour

Circles

Narrow-lined grid

Diagonal lines

Lines of zigzag side-by-side

Checkered effect with blocks of zigzag and changing scale

Repeated curved lines

Wide-lined grids

Side-to-side zigzag worked in lines

Freestyle curved lines

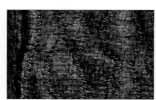

Machine-stitched cord couched in straight lines

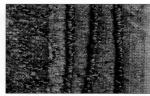

Broken lengths of zigzag placed at angles but not touching

Small-scale grid

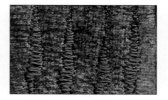

Variable-width zigzag

Zigzag worked randomly as a texture

The sample above shows various examples of the use of zigzag stitch. The key opposite explains each use in more detail.

Cable stitch

Cable stitch is good for raised lines and interesting mixes of colour can be achieved when the top and bottom threads are different colours.

Cable is worked by winding the bobbin by hand with a thicker-than-normal thread, such as cotton perle or a cotton crochet thread, and stitched from the back of the work. It can be used on fine fabric when the print has gone right through the fabric so that you can see where to stitch. Alternatively, mark the design on the back either by tacking through the edges of the print or machining around the main lines, which provide a guideline.

Whip stitch

Whip stitch is what you get when the top thread pulls the bobbin thread through to the front of the fabric and covers the top thread. Some machines are tricky to set up for whip stitch but it is worth persevering with as exciting textures can be achieved and it can give a satisfying contrast to flatter areas.

With feed dogs down or covered, and the darning foot on, the bottom tension is slackened and the top tension tightened so that the bobbin thread will be pulled through to whip the top thread. The fabric should be tightly tensioned in an embroidery frame suitable for the machine. Move the fabric slowly but run the machine fast.

Top: whip stitch embellishes a print made with corrugated card set on its edge.

Bottom: cable stitch decorates these printed circles, together with whip stitch and couched machine cords. Notice that some of the stitching follows the print and some is placed randomly over it. The danger is that the print will be completely lost if it is covered by stitching so judgement is needed to balance the stitching with the print.

This sampler show the use of cable stitch, whip stitch, tufting using a tailor's tacking foot, and machine-made cords.

Further embellishments

These are a useful addition to stitching and can liven up an otherwise dull design. But they can also be used to complement print in the same way that stitch is used. These samples show how embellishment can be used to create surface pattern, using the print as a guide.

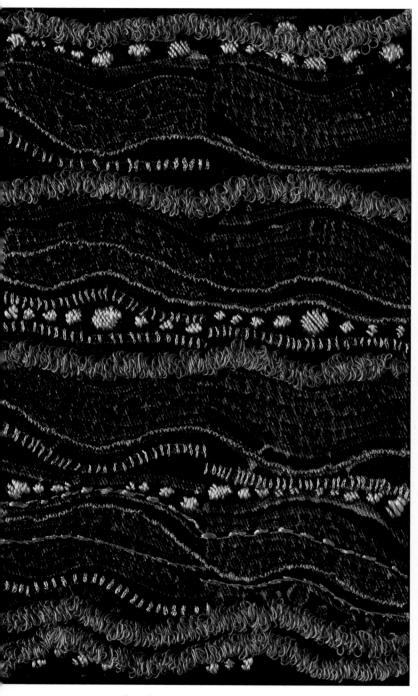

A purchased texture block is decorated with free running and a tailor's tacking foot used to create a loopy surface.

Some machines have an eyelet foot as standard, or they can be bought as an extra attachment. Eyelets are used here to decorate a bubblewrap print, creating an all-over pattern.

Conclusion

As a means of adding colour and visual texture to the surface of fabric, print offers a wide palette of easily accessible methods, from the painterly qualities of monoprint to the precise registration of repeat pattern, and the satisfaction of recycling found objects to create new images. The ability to build pattern relatively quickly is an advantage, and very subtle mixes of colour can be achieved by over-printing – dark on light, light on dark, bright colour to enliven and tertiary mixes to dull down. Adding stitch to an otherwise flat surface can transform a piece of cloth into an exciting and vibrant textile to be enjoyed just as it is or to put to any number of uses, decorative or practical. I enjoy print for its own sake as well as for the creative potential that it presents, and I hope that this introduction to print will encourage readers to make their own prints, and that both beginners and more experienced embroiderers will be inspired to explore the opportunities that come with combining the two disciplines of print with stitch.

Index